Disappearing Daughters

The Tragedy of Female Foeticide

GITA ARAVAMUDAN

PENGUIN BOOKS

PENGUIN BOOKS

Published by the Penguin Group

Penguin Books India Pvt. Ltd, 11 Community Centre, Panchsheel Park, New Delhi 110 017, India

Penguin Group (USA) Inc., 375 Hudson Street, New York, New York 10014, USA

Penguin Group (Canada), 90 Eglinton Avenue East, Suite 700, Toronto, Ontario, M4P 2Y3, Canada (a division of Pearson Penguin Canada Inc.)

Penguin Books Ltd, 80 Strand, London WC2R 0RL, England

Penguin Ireland, 25 St Stephen's Green, Dublin 2, Ireland (a division of Penguin Books Ltd)

Penguin Group (Australia), 250 Camberwell Road, Camberwell, Victoria 3124, Australia (a division of Pearson Australia Group Pty Ltd)

Penguin Group (NZ), 67 Apollo Drive, Rosedale, Auckland 0632, New Zealand (a division of Pearson New Zealand Ltd)

Penguin Group (South Africa) (Pty) Ltd, 24 Sturdee Avenue, Rosebank, Johannesburg 2196, South Africa

Penguin Books Ltd, Registered Offices: 80 Strand, London WC2R 0RL, England

First published by Penguin Books India 2007

Copyright © Gita Aravamudan 2007

ISBN   978-0143101703

Typeset in Sabon by Mantra Virtual Services, New Delhi
Printed at Repro India Ltd., Navi Mumbai

*To my husband Aravamudan and my children
Ananth, Sriram and Shuba, without whose love and
support this book could not have been written.*

Contents

Acknowledgements

I would like to begin with a very special thanks to the president of India Dr A.P.J.Abdul Kalam who gave me a message for this book. When my husband and I met President Kalam, whom we have known now for over forty years, at the Rashtrapati Bhavan, he told me to write my book quickly as female foeticide is a subject of immediate social concern.

I could not have written this book without the whole-hearted support and help I got from various NGOs, academics, field workers, journalists, doctors, administrators and ordinary people who told me their stories. I wish to thank them all.

My involvement with the subject started when I was commissioned to write an article on female infanticide for *The Week* in the early 1990s. I would like to thank T.R. Gopalakrishnan, Executive Editor of *The Week* for his encouragement and support and Chandigarh correspondent Vijaya Pushkarna and other staff members of *The Week* who provided me with contacts and information.

My special thanks are due to Andal Damodaran of the Indian Council of Child Welfare (ICCW) who helped me on my very first visit to Usilampatti in Tamil Nadu over a decade ago. Without her intervention I would not have gained access to the closed world of female infanticide. Ten years later, when I went back again to her for help, once more she gave me contacts all over the country and all of them were invariably friendly and very helpful.

From the ICCW, I would also like to thank Valli Annamalai in Madurai and Uma Rudra in Chandigarh for arranging my field trips and strengthening me with the support of their field workers.

In Ahmedabad, I would like to thank the team from Chetna who not only put me up but also cared for me in a very special way. Ila Vakaria and Bhoomika from Chetna, their colleagues and all the young people from various NGOs in Mehsana district not only took me to some of the worst affected villages in Gujarat, but also went out of their way to arrange meetings and fix rare interviews.

I would also like to specially thank:

Dr Leela Visaria, Gujarat Institute of Development Research

Dr Sabu George, researcher and activist, New Delhi

Ila Pathak, AWAG, Ahmedabad

Donna Fernandes and her colleagues from Vimochana, Bangalore

M. Jeeva and Phavalam, SIRD, Madurai

Dr S.K. Sandoo and her colleagues from the Chandigarh Family Planning Association

Dr Rainuka Dagar, IDC, Chandigarh

Radhika Batra, UNFPA, New Delhi

Dr M.D. Ravi, paediatrician, Mysore

Dr Jaya Bhat, gynaecologist, Bangalore

Dr Sarala Rajajee, paediatrician, Chennai

All of them gave me invaluable help in the form of technical input, published material, anecdotal information and contacts. They shared their field experiences with me and gave me their publications which were a great source of information.

Foreword

The author states that an enlightened doctor can never be a conspirer of female foeticide and indeed the medical practitioner should be the protector of the child from its formation, through its birth and growth. To enable the doctors to always remember their responsibility to society, I suggest, that while entering the medical profession, all students completing the medical degree may be asked to take the following oath:

'I promise to society and to my parents that I will protect every human life in formation or in birth.'

The author also suggests that both the society and the Government should project the girl child as a social asset. While agreeing, my thoughts are:

Is not the grandmother a social asset?

Is not the mother a social asset?

Is not the daughter a social asset?

Is not the homemaker a social asset?

On planet Earth, Woman is indeed the Almighty's gift. I would like to narrate a story on the creation of humans. Almighty God worked for millions of years to design and evolve an image. He went on looking at the image and improved and improved upon it. He finally decided to give it life. He looked at the galaxies and the oceans and finally looked at his own creation—Man. As soon as Man got life, two things happened. First, he opened his eyes and smiled. God was happy. Next, he opened his mouth and said, 'Almighty, thank you.' God was very happy. He was delighted to see His creation and felt that His creation did the two right things.

Then He found something missing in His creation. He then created fire in the flash of a second, out of which came Saithan (Great Devil). God told Saithan to prostrate before His best creation—Man—and pay his respects. Saithan said, 'Oh God, you took millions of years to create Man. But you created me out of fire in the flash of a second. So, I am the best.' The Almighty, who had created the universe with mighty orbiting galaxies with orbiting stars and planets, was bewildered with this response of Saithan. He had created the best of His creation, Man, on one side, and on another side, Saithan, probably the worst. He thought of it and looked at both with benevolence. The Almighty then integrated Man and Saithan and told Man, 'Now since you have been blessed with thinking faculties your vision has to beat the Saithan within you and reach Me.' Then, God decided Man would become cruel unless he created a companion. That is why Woman was created to be a partner to Man in his struggle to overcome ignorance and acquire knowledge. As Rumi said:

'Angel is free because of his knowledge,
The beast because of his ignorance,
Between the two remains the son of man to struggle.'

Woman will elevate Man to higher levels that are angelic. Mrs Gita Aravamudan's book, with case studies from various states of our country, is indeed an important contribution for promoting good societal life. The book touches our conscience. I am sure the author's effort will lead to a social debate on this important topic resulting in the formulation of solutions. It may help to check the misconception and the unthinking misuse of technology by educated families and by the medical community.

Rashtrapati Bhavan
New Delhi
31 May 2006   A.P.J. Abdul Kalam

Preface

When I embarked on writing this book, to me, female foeticide was what we in journalistic parlance call 'a story'. To track this story I decided to use the only tools I knew: the old fashioned tools of investigative reporting.

I knew it would require patience, doggedness and a lot of probing. Getting people to confide in me would not be easy. Wherever I went, I would be an outsider. There was plenty of research data available on the subject, but somewhere along the line the human face had gone missing. I knew that my story would not emerge easily. What I did not really expect was the momentum the story would gather.

As the months rolled by, I found that the story of *Disappearing Daughters* became bigger than any story I had ever done before. It had so many facets to it. So many frightening aspects and so many tragic fallouts.

I had investigated female infanticide in Tamil Nadu earlier and I knew how difficult and dangerous it was to pry into very personal and frightening secrets. However, the crime of daughters being killed *after they were born* paled before the much more widespread crime of daughters being killed even *while they were in the womb*.

Female infanticide is akin to serial killing. But female

foeticide was more like a holocaust. A whole gender is getting exterminated. It is a silent and smoothly executed crime which leaves no waves in its wake. It is happening while we, as a nation, slumber. In some parts of the country almost two generations of women have been exterminated before I completed this book and there is still no solution in sight.

As a journalist, I can only narrate the story. I have no solutions to offer. A finger in the dyke can help to stem a trickle. But even the best dykes in the world have to be fortified to tackle a deluge.

Maybe this narration will help. Maybe it will touch the right chords in places where it matters. And maybe . . . just maybe . . . we might come up with something more than a finger in the dyke.

In Search of Disappearing Daughters

'We have to be careful,' the car driver said. 'We are going into dangerous territory. The Kallars are violent people. They won't hesitate to cut you up with an *aruval*, stuff the pieces into a sack and chuck it off a rocky cliff.' He gave a dramatic pause. 'And no one will ever know what happened to you.'

A collective tremor went through the car. Rocky hills loomed on either side of the tarred road on which we were travelling. I shuddered thinking of the sacks of bones that could be lying there among the thorn bushes. Should I turn around and go back to the warm security of Madurai?

The year was 1994. I was on my way to Usilampatti in the Madurai district of Tamil Nadu on a strange and scary mission. I wanted to find out if mothers really killed their newborn girl babies in this area.

For some years now, an alarming number of baby girls had been disappearing without a trace in the Madurai, Salem and Dharmapuri districts of Tamil Nadu. The suspicion was that they had been killed by their own families.

This terrible secret behind their disappearance came to light for the first time in December 1985, when the popular Tamil magazine *Junior Vikatan* published an article on the killing of girl babies in Usilampatti. The readers were shocked. They had heard grandmothers' tales of girl babies being killed by their own families. But no one really believed it was still happening. And yet this magazine said that girl babies were being killed right under their noses.

The title of the article was very specific: '*Varadatchinaikku Bayandhu Penn Kuzhandhaigalai Kolgirargal*' (Fearing dowry they kill girl babies). Six months later, the English magazine *India Today* literally dug for the truth and came up with another chilling article complete with gruesome pictures of infant skeletons. According to that article 'Born to Die', the girl babies had been killed by their own families and buried in shallow makeshift graves in their backyards.

The government woke up. So did the local politicians, the NGOs and the Tamil and national press.

The government went into denial. Copies of the magazines were burnt in public. Politicians claimed the articles had tarnished the reputation of the villagers and hounded the activists who were responsible for getting the press down to Usilampatti. The activists were even summoned to the police station. By then Usilampatti caught the attention of the national media. A spate of articles appeared. Even the BBC did a programme on killer mothers.

Meanwhile, alarm bells were sounding in other directions. As early as 1990, even before the shocking 1991 decennial census figures for India were out, noted economist Amartya Sen had said that there were 'more than 10 million women missing in South Asia, West Asia and North Africa'. He was referring to the large deficit of girl babies in these parts of the world. It was suspected that quite a large percentage of these 'missing' women might belong to India. 'These numbers,' he said, 'tell us, quietly, a terrible story of inequality and neglect leading to the excess mortality of women.'[1]

One year later, the new census figures indicated that the figures were even more alarming than most experts had imagined. The sex ratios in almost every state had dipped. Sex selective abortion, which had raised its ugly head in the big cities in the mid 1980s, had already had a devastating effect on urban populations.

One study, for example, indicated that in Jaipur, capital of Rajasthan, prenatal sex determination tests resulted in the abortions of about 3500 female foetuses annually. The UNICEF reported that a 1984 study on abortions after prenatal sex determination in Mumbai found that 7999 out of 8000 of the aborted foetuses were females. 'Sex determination,' the UNICEF report stated, 'has become a lucrative business.'[2]

Ironically, these alarm bells were largely ignored. The more lurid practice of killing infant girl babies grabbed more headlines, at least for a while. But soon even the press lost interest and the ripples created by the articles faded away. Eight years had passed. Girl babies continued to disappear in Usilampatti. Everyone knew where they were going and how they were killed and yet, not a single killer parent had been arrested.

The NGOs had made only a marginal impact. At the same time, stories of infanticide began surfacing from Salem and Dharmapuri areas. In 1992, under Chief Minister J. Jayalalitha, the state government launched a 'Cradle Babies' scheme. The cradles were kept in government primary health centres and in 'Collection Centres' run by NGOs like the Indian Council for Child Welfare (ICCW). NGOs were given funds to look after the 'unwanted' baby girls left in the cradles. In that year alone, seventy-seven babies were left in government cradles in Salem district. Unfortunately only twenty survived and they were given for adoption. In Usilampatti, the scheme proved even less popular and soon had to be abandoned.

By 1994, it had become evident that *penn sissu kolai* or female infanticide was a well-entrenched social practice in many communities across Tamil Nadu. Thanks to monitoring by voluntary organizations, more accurate figures were now available and they were quite staggering.

The original magazine article in *Junior Vikatan* said that in 1986, out of 600 female births registered in the Usilampatti taluk hospital, 570 babies had disappeared and most of them were suspected to be victims of infanticide. Eight years and many studies later, social workers in the area said that those figures might have been exaggerated. But the figures were still bad enough. The detailed records maintained by ICCW showed that in their project area, out of 1194 female babies born between April and December 1993, 156 were suspected to have been killed, 243 infanticides were prevented and just seven babies were left in the cradle.

The ICCW project was started in 1987. In the beginning it covered just about five villages. By 1994 288 villages came under its ambit. There were several other NGOs working in the area. One with deep roots in the community itself was the Society for Integrated Rural Development (SIRD), which was started by Jeeva and Devamanohar, two lawyers from the Kallar community. In fact, SIRD had been instrumental in bringing the first journalists to Usilampatti in 1986.

In January 1994, an arrest was finally made. Karupayee of Kattukarukanpatti village in the Usilampatti taluk of Madurai district was arrested for killing her infant daughter. According to newspaper reports, the ICCW team had been monitoring this woman who already had two living daughters. Two other baby girls had died soon after they were born to her. They suspected that this child would also be killed if it turned out to be a girl. So they kept vigil over her hut and took her to the Usilampatti Government hospital when she went into labour. There, Karupayee gave birth to her fifth daughter. The baby was quite healthy and weighed 3.5 kg.

However, the next morning both mother and child were missing from the hospital. When the Project Director of ICCW, Jayanthi, went to Karupayee's house the next morning to give her the nutrition chart and other relevant information, she found the child missing. The mother failed to give her a convincing reply when she asked to see the baby.

Frustrated, Jayanthi lodged a complaint with the Usilampatti police and Karupayee was arrested for causing suspicious death. Surprisingly, for once, the police had acted promptly. Karupayee and her husband Karuthakannan confessed that the infant had been buried right in front of their house. The tiny body was exhumed and subjected to a post-mortem at the Madurai Medical College. The medical report showed that the neck of the baby had been compressed and the bone was broken to pieces. In other words the just-born infant had been strangled to death.

As I read through the reports again, I found it difficult to believe that parents could kill their own child in such a violent manner. But ever since I started on this quest, people have told me of the various horrifying ways in which girl babies were 'traditionally' put to death. Mothers and grandmothers sometimes fed a just-born girl with a drop of milk laced with the crushed seeds of the poisonous oleander. Or they would feed the baby a spoon of castor oil with a single husk of paddy, which slit her delicate throat as it slid in. A drop of the poisonous milky sap of the oleander would also do the deed. The more 'scientific' minded would drop a few sleeping pills or a bit of pesticide into the milk.

Killing girl children also seemed to be a kind of pan national 'tradition'. In Gujarat, I was told mothers would drown their newborn daughters in milk and in Punjab they would bury them alive in sealed mud pots. Mothers obviously killed, and they killed cruelly. And now, here at last was solid evidence that it was still happening.

I was on my way to Usilampatti to see if I could trace Karupayee's family or Jayanthi the social worker, or anyone else who would tell me about this gruesome practice as it existed in Tamil Nadu. I had my apprehensions. The Kallars, a proud and militant race, were the dominant community here. In fact they had been branded a 'criminal' community by the British and once upon a time, under a special act, all their able-bodied young men were required to spend their nights at the police station. They would not want an outsider coming and probing into their deepest and darkest secrets. How did I even imagine I would be able to break through the barriers of silence with which they had shrouded themselves? A shiver went down my spine. Would I end up as another sack of bones?

My first stop at the Usilampatti government hospital proved to be fruitless. No one seemed to be in charge. More importantly, no one wanted to talk; especially about *penn sissu kolai*. The few women I spoke to outside the hospital gave me hostile glares, while their menfolk twirled their impressive moustaches and asked me to go away and not spread such lies.

'See, this is a girl,' one man said, aggressively pushing a four year old in front of my nose. 'She is my daughter. She is alive isn't she?'

His wife stood behind him holding a newborn.

'And this one?' I asked touching it.

'A boy,' she said timidly. 'Thank God, he is a boy.'

'I think we should leave,' the driver muttered as we got into the car. 'These people are hiding something and they don't want to be questioned. If they get angry . . .'

He left it unsaid this time.

I spent several more days in Usilampatti, but I never met Karupayee or her family. She was in prison and the area in which she lived was bristling with tension. I did, however, meet Jayanthi and her team of young women who bravely went into the villages and saved girl babies from certain death. They were the ones who introduced me to a topsy-turvy world where mothers killed their own daughters because they did not want them 'to suffer', and where grandmothers fed poison to their own flesh and blood so that they could make space for more sons in the family. Could family planning become more macabre?

Over the years Karupayee's case, with all its twists and turns, became to me symbolic of the many, many things I did not know or understand about the devastating effect of patriarchy on disempowered women. And, of the retrograde effect law enforcement could have on their already miserable lives.

When a woman killed her own daughter, who was the victim and who the perpetrator? As the days went by, this seemingly simple question spiralled into a vortex of unanswerables. I didn't know then that I was standing on the brink of a chasm. To me, at that moment of time, female infanticide was the most unspeakable of crimes. I didn't realize it appeared gruesome because of its potential visual impact. It appeared unspeakable because in my mind, the killing of an infant was akin to murder. I didn't realize then how much more lethal and how much more devastating the unseen, 'less messy' crime of female foeticide could be.

And yet, it was an illiterate, disempowered woman named Lakshmi who pointed out to me a fact which had been staring me in the face all along, but which I had chosen to ignore. How did it matter how the girl child was killed, she asked me. The rich could afford scans and abortions, but did that make the killing more forgivable? At that point of time her anguished statement opened my eyes just a bit. But as the years rolled by and I delved further into the murky issue of the massacre of females, the moral dilemma her statement posed kept rising over and over again.

I met Lakshmi in Alligundam village. It was the ICCW team who took me to Alligundam. After my failure at the Government hospital, I went in search of Jayanthi. I located her at the office-cum-crèche of the ICCW in one of the bylanes of Usilampatti .

Jayanthi turned out to be a brisk young woman in her mid-twenties. She and her colleagues, who were all unmarried women in their twenties, divided their time between caring for the abandoned babies, counselling the villagers and actively preventing parents from killing their infant daughters.

At first Jayanthi was unwilling to talk. Her intervention in Karupayee's case had caused a backlash. Now she and her colleagues faced even more hostility from the villagers. It took a lot of persuasion and a phone call from Madras (now Chennai) to get her to agree to co-operate. Finally, she agreed to send one of her colleagues with me to visit some of the worst hit villages.

And so, there I was standing outside Lakshmi's mud hut in Alligundam village, a couple of kilometers away from the Usilampatti taluk headquarters. At first glance, Alligundam appeared almost idyllic. The road leading to the village was flanked by lush green paddy fields. We parked our vehicle under a huge tree next to the village temple. The serenity was striking. How could anyone who lived here ever kill an infant?

But it was a deceptive serenity, which lasted for hardly a couple of minutes. Within moments we were surrounded by a group of militant looking young men who had been sitting under the tree playing cards. Obviously they knew the woman who came with me. They started jeering at her and throwing insults at us, but she seemed used to it and just looked straight ahead and did not reply.

'Oh, you have come with one more town person,' one man said to her as he fingered the chopper hanging around his hip. 'Have you not had enough? Why do you keep coming and interfering in our lives? What do you people know about poverty or how tough it is to be a woman in this society?'

'You people from the town come and spread lies about us,' another one said. 'You tarnish the name of our villages.'

An old man with an awesome moustache came and stood close to us. 'Who said we kill our female babies?' he demanded. 'Go. Go into the village and see for yourself. See how many girls there are.'

They didn't prevent us from going in, but followed us making rude comments and laughing as we crossed the stream of dirty water gurgling through the main lane. We picked up our contact Navaneetham from one of the huts. Navaneetham belonged to the village but even she was being ostracized because she helped the 'town people'.

Navaneetham kept track of the pregnant women in the 'high risk' group. The 'high risk' group I learnt consisted of women who already had one or more daughters. They were the ones most likely to kill the next child if it were a girl. Jayanthi had explained to me that having one girl was okay because a girl was needed to 'light the lamp' in the house. But more than one was not desirable.

Lakshmi was definitely in the high risk group because she

had a four-year-old living daughter and had lost her next daughter, soon after she was born, under suspicious circumstances. Now they were keeping a close vigil over her.

Lakshmi turned out to be a thin young woman in her early twenties. She was dressed in a faded cotton sari. Her seven-month pregnancy bulged out of her scrawny frame as she sat combing her daughter's hair. Her father-in-law stood at the doorway, glowering at us.

As we stood in front of Lakshmi's house trying to talk to her, the whole village seemed to be standing around us watching and listening.

'*Amma thaaye*, go away. Leave me alone,' Lakshmi said, not looking at us. 'I beg you leave me alone. What do you want from me? What power do you think I have over my womb? None. Do I have any right to decide if I can keep this child if it is a girl? No. So why do you bother me?'

'Look at her,' one of the young men interjected. 'If she has one more girl what will she do? Think of all the expenses. Think of the clothes she will have to buy, the jewellery she will have to make. Think of the coming of age ceremony she will have to perform, the *varadatchinai* and *seer varisai* she will have to give. Where do you think the money will come from? One girl is bad enough . . .'

So, was the answer death? I asked turning to look at him.

He shrugged. He was a tough looking young man with bulging biceps. 'That is for her family to decide,' he said. 'Not you people.'

'Better to kill her before she knows this miserable life,' said an old woman, squatting on the mud path in front of her hut watching the fun. She shaded her rheumy eyes with her hand as she looked up at me. 'Better to send her straight to heaven rather than make her endure this beating and kicking around. What joy have we got by staying alive?'

'You shut up *paati* [grandma],' one of the men said laughing. 'Otherwise this lady will say you have killed all your daughters and put you into prison.'

That is when Lakshmi made her thought-provoking statement. 'It is all very well for you town people to speak,' she said. 'You can afford to have yourself tested by machines and kill the girl child even when it is in the womb. In what way is that less of a crime? Is that not also killing? Has any town woman been arrested for that?'

We moved on followed by our little procession. In a tiny mud hut at the furthest end of the village lived sixty-year-old Kanchamma, the village midwife, who had brought hundreds of babies to life and sent several of them back to their maker. Kanchamma lay on a cot nursing the head wound she had received from her neighbour's aruval. She was a wiry small-built woman, dark and wizened beyond her years.

Kanchamma was a bit wary about speaking to me as the group of men who had followed me now stood menacingly around her. But, she was a brave woman. After all she had dared to argue with a man wielding an aruval.

Yes, she said, there were many who did not want girl children and they had ways and means of disposing of them. Of course she had seen many girl children being 'sent away' but she had no means of preventing it.

'Careful, careful,' someone warned her. 'Careful about what you say. You may be arrested.'

'She herself is responsible for many deaths,' the social worker beside me muttered. 'But she cannot admit it or she will be put into prison like Karupayee.'

I wanted to speak to Kanchamma alone. She ordered the people crammed into the hut to leave and very reluctantly they trooped out. Thus finally, secure in the privacy of her dark hut, Kanchamma whispered her awful secrets to me. It was almost as if she was waiting to unburden herself to someone. The stories came tumbling out. She spoke with graphic gestures, sometimes enacting the scenes that had taken place. It was eerie how she could speak so calmly about death and killing.

'Now they no longer feed them the paddy husk or the poisoned milk,' she was saying. 'They stifle them with a pillow or with a cloth. Oh! It is a horrible sight. The little one will struggle under the sari like this, like this,' she simulated an infant struggling for its life under the sari. 'And then it will be still. Oh! How many I have seen.'

But why did she not do anything to stop it?

'Who am I?' she asked, almost sadly. 'What right do I have? I am only paid to do a job. It is my livelihood. It is their child and their wish. I have kept all my daughters. But if they want to send theirs away . . .'

'She is not as innocent as she would want you to believe,' the social worker remarked when I came out and told her a little bit of what Kanchamma had said. 'The parents rarely kill the child themselves. They pay her to do it. She is paid to deliver the child and also to kill it if it is a girl. Sometimes they ask her to give away the child and she does that too.'

Over the next few days, as we rattled through dusty village roads and crossed paddy fields to visit remote hamlets, I began to understand the enormity of the problem these women faced. As Karuthamma, the mother of three sons, told me, women had no rights and no power to decide.

Karuthamma lived in a nondescript village in Chellampatti block. To reach the village we had to walk through paddy fields and up a mud track. The nearest bus stop was more than two kilometres away.

Karuthamma was in her early thirties. She must have been

beautiful once but several childbirths and toiling hard in the fields had taken their toll on her. She came under the high risk group because she was pregnant again, and was also about to become a grandmother. Her fifteen-year-old daughter Shanthi was pregnant with her first child. Shanthi was her first and only living daughter.

'I do not want any more children, but my husband and in-laws will not let me have a family planning operation,' she said. She was sitting outside her house scrubbing the pots they had used for cooking the morning meal. 'I told them I have given you three sons what more do you want. But they will not agree. I have already given birth to six children.'

But only four of them were alive. What happened to the rest?

'They died,' she said in a matter of fact manner. 'They were girls.' She refused to say anything more about them. About her daughter she said, 'She too will give birth to ten children and still have no *vurumai* (right) over her own body. Her body will become tired like mine. I wanted to send her to school, but I was forced to get her married as soon as she came of age. Now look at her fate. It is the same as mine.'

To Karuthamma the town was a far away and inaccessible place. Even if she decided to have a family planning operation, she had neither the means nor the money to go to the town. If she sought the help of the social workers she would be beaten and stigmatized. If getting permission to go to the 'town' was unthinkable, imagine getting permission for a family planning operation. But there were a few brave and enterprising women too, like Chinnathayee.

Chinnathayee was a widow in her early forties. Her two grown up sons had married and left home. When her fifteen-year-old daughter Janaki gave birth to twin daughters in the Usilampatti General Hospital the girl's in-laws rejected her for her 'crime'. Since the babies were weak and underweight, many of their relatives and even other patients in the maternity ward advised Janaki to do away with at least one of them.

But Chinnathayee, supported by the social workers, was determined to keep them alive. She knew how traumatizing killing a girl baby could be. As I sat in her hut listening to her story, she pointed to an innocuous looking *ammi* (grinding stone) in a corner of her cooking area.

'Look at that,' she said. 'It is one of the "treasures" my mother-in-law left me. It has been passed down for generations in my husband's family. I don't know how many deaths it has been responsible for. I don't know how many generations of girl babies have been poisoned by the seeds ground on that stone.'

Obviously Chinnathayee must have lost a few girl babies too though she did not want to talk about it. She just said she was determined that no more girl babies would die in her home. So, instead of just 'letting' Janaki's babies die as her friend and relatives advised her, she decided to make them live. She took them to Madurai and got them treated in the government hospital. Her neighbours chuckled as they remembered how she brought her tiny granddaughters home from Madurai by bus, carrying them in a cloth shopping bag.

Now Janaki's husband was visiting her again. His neighbours had convinced him that the girl was still young enough to give him a number of sons. There was no guarantee of course that her next child would be a son. And there was no guarantee that her next daughter, if and when she was born, would be allowed to live. But for the moment, two baby girls had come out of their ordeal alive thanks to their brave grandmother.

Thus by the end of the week, though I had not met

Karupayee herself, I had actually met a hundred Karupayees: victims of a system which left them with no control even over the most intimate parts of their bodies. Even the social workers who were responsible for Karupayee's arrest were not sure if they had done the right thing. For after all, she was in reality a victim and not a perpetrator.

At the SIRD office, Jeeva and Devamanoharan gave me a surprising new insight. It was not poverty per se but the unequal distribution of prosperity that had led to the spread of female infanticide in the Kallar community said.

The Kallars were originally a nomadic tribe who probably came from north India. They were a militant warrior people who never hesitated to take a life. Some historical records indicated that even as far back as the early nineteenth century, girl babies were being killed in the community. However, few had imagined that this practice would become so widespread after Independence. The systematic elimination of girl children could be traced to the rise of commercialization and the subsequent marginalization of the women in the community. And this, said Jeeva, happened with the building of the famous Vaigai dam.

Ironically, the Vaigai irrigation project, which was supposed to have brought prosperity to the area and stability into the lives of the Kallar community, resulted in the large-scale elimination of women. As long as the Kallar men were on the move, the women were in charge of their meagre lands and of the families. The Vaigai project created some arable lands on which the Kallar community was settled by the government. This was supposed to put an end to their violent nomadic life and give them a settled existence.

This apparently was the first move which curtailed the independence of the Kallar women. Once the men came back and settled down, they pushed the women back into their traditional cooking and child-bearing roles. They were completely blocked from taking part in any economic activities.

Unfortunately, the lands were not all equally fertile. The irrigation project created a wet fertile area and a dry area where nothing grew. The wetland farmers became more prosperous as they began going in for cash crops. They were soon exposed to the commercialized practices of the outside world. The dry land farmers eked out a living. This disparity disrupted traditional family and marriage bonds.

Then the wetland farmers stumbled upon one more lucrative proposition: *varadatchinai* (dowry). The Kallars as a community normally married amongst themselves. Jeeva said that not so long ago, dowry was unheard of among the Kallars as the men had to pay a bride price. Marriages were simple and mostly arranged within the extended joint family. However, now the wetland farmers demanded dowry from the families from the dry area who wished to buy their way into a more coveted lifestyle. Along with *varadatchinai* came other practices which further commodified the women.

Seer varisai, for instance, is the traditional dowry given in kind by the girl's maternal uncle on a couple of important occasions during her lifetime. This had now become a status symbol. The men were demanding more *seer* and on more and more occasions. Devamanoharan said the practice had become so pernicious that men were demanding *seer* from their wives' people even when they went on a pilgrimage. Even a casual labourer wanted Rs 10, 000 as dowry and a grand wedding complete with video coverage. Trapped in this double bind, the women had no way out. They could question neither the barter which took place using their bodies nor the killing of the girl babies they produced.

Jeeva recalled his first face-to-face encounter with female

infanticide. In the mid-1980s, about two years after starting SIRD, he was taking classes for children in a tiny village called Kalloothu in Usilampatti district. His colleague Rohini Devi, who was taking night classes for adults some distance away, suddenly came running to him, her eyes flashing with anger and tears pouring down her cheeks.

'They are killing a girl child,' she cried.

He ran with her to the house where the incident was taking place and found a female infant lying on the mud floor, its limbs twitching. She was in the final throes of death. The infant, he learnt, had been fed the milk of a poisonous plant. All the women in the house were wailing loudly as they watched the child die. That was a moment of truth for Jeeva. He realized that female infanticide was not a myth but something which really happened.

Later on the SIRD members talked about it at their monthly meeting. They discussed the underlying causes and came to the conclusion that *varadatchinai* and *seer varasai* were the primary reasons behind the devaluation of women.

'The value of a woman goes down every time the value of gold goes up,' Thayamma a fifty-year-old grandmother in Alligundam had told me a few days ago. 'Who does this gold benefit?'

And she could not have been more right. The gold that was given to a woman at the time of her marriage certainly did not benefit her in any way. It was used by her menfolk for their own needs. It was used by her husband's family as a whip to force her to bring more from her natal home. It was used as the noose to snuff out the lives of the girl children she would bear. To the women of the Kallar community now, the killing of girl children had almost become an act of compassion. It was as if they were freeing their daughters from the hardships they would otherwise have to face.

So, why did families still kill the babies? Why did they not leave their daughters in the cradles at the orphanage? Or give them away in adoption? The cradle to them symbolized all that could go wrong. Some of the babies left in the cradles had died. But more importantly, the families were suspicious of government schemes. If another government came into power or funds ran out, what would happen to the babies they had left in the cradles, they asked.

'Better to send my daughter to her maker than to leave her to the mercy of an *anaadhashram* [orphanage],' said Kamakshi a strong-looking woman in her twenties who had just come in from the fields.

Kamakshi was pregnant with her third child. Her two-year-old daughter and four-year-old son were being fed *kanji* (rice gruel) by her mother-in-law. She stroked her round stomach. 'Even if this one is a daughter, I will never leave her in the cradle. Today she may be a baby but tomorrow she will grow up into a young woman and who knows how the orphanage will use her?'

Kamakshi obviously was a fairly independent-minded woman. Sadly, she had totally internalized the 'need' to kill girl babies. She spoke boldly of the fear which haunted the disempowered mothers who killed their daughters. What would happen to these innocent lives when they flowered into womanhood? Who would trample on them and crush them into the same nothingness? It could be the unseen disembodied authorities into whose hands they entrusted their precious daughters. Or it could be the men and women in their own families. So why let them grow, only to be hacked down again, she demanded almost aggressively.

Over the next couple of years, Karupayee's tragedy took on new dimensions. Although she perhaps was not personally responsible for killing her infant daughter, she took the blame on herself and was put into prison, where she delivered one more daughter. By the time she was released from prison, a couple of years later, she had come to symbolize all that was wrong with this kind of approach.

2

Who is the Victim?

' A s soon as the baby girl was born, my mother-in-law kicked it with her toe and said, "Who wants this?" She wrapped it in a wet towel and left it on the floor. My husband's sister, weak after the delivery, just wept. It died within a few hours.'

Palaniamma from Nalampalli was describing the birth and death of her sister-in-law's third daughter: the unnamed, unacknowledged girl child who was killed by her own grandmother. An infant whose death had been ordered by her own father because she was not the son he wanted.

The year was 1999. I was in Salem, listening to a horrifying story of slaughter. Palaniamma's third daughter, her other sister-in-law's fourth daughter, her neighbour's second daughter . . . The list was awesome, and the methods of killing increasingly cruel. According to figures collected by the Tamil Nadu government from primary health centres in the area, at least 3000 infants had been killed in Dharmapuri district of Tamil Nadu in the last three years.

Four years had passed since my first visit to Usilampatti. Four years since Karupayee was first arrested. Things had improved quite dramatically in Usilampatti. The number of recorded female infanticides had gone down from 181 in 1994 to just 22 in 1997 according to the ICCW records.

However, in Dharmapuri, one of the worst affected areas, 105 baby girls were still being killed on an average every month in 1997. The government figures indicated that most of these deaths occurred in Pennagaram block where the female literacy was just 31.3 per cent, well below the state average of 41.8 per cent. In Pennagaram alone, three infant girls were killed every day.

Newborn girls were disappearing here and in some pockets they were disappearing really fast. In one locality of Salem district, there were just 200 girls for 400 boys in the below seven age group. In 22 villages around a radius of 10 kms the total number of girls was just 4330 as against 6224 boys. In fact, in several villages in this area the sex ratio was around two boys to every girl.

If the killing was quick and relatively painless in1994 in Usilampatti, it was prolonged and torturous now in Dharmapuri. The tiny infants were not killed instantaneously but their bodies were deliberately weakened and dehydrated by their own parents.

'Now they are afraid of detection,' said Alphonso Mary, a public health nurse who had brought Palaniamma to Salem.

Alphonso Mary was a woman with a mission. For over a decade now, this simple bespectacled woman had been tirelessly going around the villages, visiting houses, pleading with women to keep their daughters. She could be aggressive or cajoling. Many times she failed to get her message through and the baby was killed. But she was never disheartened. She never gave up, because, she said, there were so many other times when she was able to save a baby.

Although Alphonso Mary was not from this locality, she knew everything about the women amongst whom she lived. She knew of their fears and their problems and could sense when a woman was going to kill her baby no matter what anyone said. She also knew they trusted her because she would never get them arrested. Ironically, the fear of arrest had not acted as a deterrent in Dharmapuri. It had only made the families adopt more torturous methods of killing.

'If someone registers a case of suspected infanticide and the body is exhumed, the "old" methods of killing can be detected,' Mary said. 'They still kill. But they are more careful and more secretive.'

Female infanticide I found had become more 'scientific'. Inducing pneumonia was the modern method. The infant was wrapped in a wet towel or dipped in cold water as soon as it was born or when it came back home from hospital. If, after a couple of hours, it was still alive it was taken to a doctor who would diagnose pneumonia and prescribe medicine, which the parents promptly threw away. When the child finally died, the parents had a medical certificate to prove pneumonia. Sometimes the infant was fed a drop of alcohol to create diarrhoea: another 'certifiable disease'.

The question now was how should the law enforcing authorities react to this slaughter of innocent infants? Should the mothers who killed their baby daughters be given capital punishment? Should they be imprisoned at all? Were they really the guilty ones?

Karupayee's arrest and subsequent imprisonment had raised these questions which still remained unanswered. In a way, Karupayee's arrest was a watershed event. In the Usilampatti area it had had a kind of salutary effect. Women no longer openly spoke of killing their babies. And willy nilly, the number of infant deaths had come down.

But in Salem and Dharmapuri, the story was very different. Avoiding detection had now become as important as the killing itself. The infants were sometimes cremated, but that aroused suspicion because the usual practice was burial. Cases had been booked against parents who killed their babies. Some had been arrested. Others were out on bail. However, it seemed as if only the weakest and the most vulnerable were the victims. The ones who killed and got caught were often abysmally poor and ignorant. Those with economic or social clout got away scot-free.

At Kolisanahalli, for example, I met Muniamma and Krishnan who eked out a living as agricultural labourers. A case of female infanticide has been registered against them by the Panchayat vice-president and the president of the local Nehru Yuvak Kendra. The couple, who were now out on bail, had two living daughters.

Muniamma's third daughter was the one who died suspiciously soon after birth. A post-mortem examination of the body, which was exhumed a couple of weeks prior to my visit, had revealed that the baby had been given a sedative, a benign but detectable way of killing. The question now was what would happen to the couple's two daughters if they were given capital punishment or even imprisoned for several years.

'In Devarsampettai, the Oor Gounder, who is the most important man in the village, killed his female infant,' a village health nurse told me. 'Infanticide cuts across all castes and communities and knows no economic barriers.'

This was a shocking revelation, but one which was authenticated by detailed data collected from a government sponsored survey of rural households in Tamil Nadu. The survey was the brainchild of Sheela Rani Chunkath, a dynamic bureaucrat who launched an aggressive campaign to tackle the problem when she was the Tamil Nadu Commissioner for Maternal and Child Health and Welfare. Using evidence collected from the records of the Primary Health Centres (PHCs) in the state, her team put together a comprehensive picture of the problem in Tamil Nadu.

The survey indicated that the 'female infanticide belt' in Tamil Nadu stretched through the districts of Salem, Dharmapuri, North Arcot, Periyar, Dindigul and Madurai. The hardcore regions were in north Salem, south Dharmapuri, south Dindigul and west Madurai. These blocks accounted for practically 70 per cent of all female infanticides in Tamil Nadu in 1995.

The survey also revealed that female infanticide was not confined to the Kallar community in Madurai and the Gounders in Salem as it was originally believed. It was prevalent among thirty-five 'self-ascribed' caste groups in Dindigul and the Thevars, Vanniars, Pariyars and Pallars in other areas. The Kallars and Gounders, because of their 'numerical and social' dominance were believed to have initiated and legitimized this practice, which gained widespread acceptability especially among the poor.

In Bandanahalli near Dharmapuri, nurse Tulasi had collected a group of women in the health centre. Some of them had sent a baby or two 'to the military' as they euphemistically called it. They spoke about it without any emotion. Valli, now pregnant with her eighth child, crouched in a corner. She refused to tell us how two of her baby girls had died.

'Are you *thai ammas* (mothers) or *nai ammas* (bitches)?' nurse Alphonso Mary cried angrily. 'How can you kill your own babies?'

In the group was a child welfare officer who worked for the Tamil Nadu Integrated Nutrition Project. Tulasi suspected her and her husband, who was also a government employee, of killing their second daughter. They already had a living son and daughter.

'The baby was perfectly healthy when she was born in the

health centre. An hour later she went home. The next morning the child was dead,' Tulasi said. 'Look at her now, how unrepentant she is!'

But the woman was defiant. 'Prove it,' she shouted angrily, 'You people just conclude that whenever a baby girl dies it is infanticide. The child died because it was unwell.' Like most couples in the area, she and her husband would not go in for a family planning operation on the pretext that it might make them 'weak'. The truth was they did not want to stop with just one son.

To help them with this aspiration, one more modern convenience has found its way into these villages—the ubiquitous scan. Muthulakshmi of Jagadevi village told me she had paid Rs 250 for a sex determination scan in Krishnagiri. Even though she was six months pregnant, the doctor had offered her an abortion when she found out it was a girl.

'But I couldn't afford it,' Muthulakshmi admitted ruefully. Four-month-old Ramya, her fifth daughter, was being closely monitored by Valiammal, the village health nurse.

A case had been registered against a leading gynaecologist in Krishnagiri. According to the charge sheet, the scan report issued by this doctor to a woman (who later died because of an abortion performed in another clinic) clearly stated it was for sex determination. This contravened the pre-natal diagnostic techniques (regulation and prevention of misuse) act of 1994. The doctor however, had been able to avoid arrest because her husband had a lot of political clout.

My experiences at Usilampatti and Salem were like a prelude to a deluge. They opened my eyes to the fact that families would do anything to have more sons. If this meant killing off all the girl children who were born, they would do that too. But, at that point I was under the delusion that killing of daughters was restricted to the poor and illiterate doubly disempowered women who had no control over their lives. Hence, the solution to this seemed simple enough. Educate and empower the women and they would stop killing their own babies. This was the approach of most of the NGOs who entered the arena around that time.

The credit for curbing female infanticide in many areas of Usilampatti goes largely to the ICCW, whose teams worked steadily despite several setbacks. In the late 1980s, when they started their first crèche project in one of the villages, they were almost hounded out.

During one of my visits I met Valli Annamalai, the secretary of the ICCW project, who lives in Madurai. She recalled those early days in the 1980s, when her team members who were mostly young women were invariably greeted with loud jeers and vulgar comments whenever they entered a village. Unemployed young men sitting around at the village entrance would assume threatening postures and ask them to leave. The women were terrified but they persisted.

Since they were pioneers in this area, they did not have any specific precedents to follow or experience to fall back upon. They did not belong to the villages and so were always considered 'outsiders' even though they spoke the same language. Valli and her team decided the only way to reach the women was through the children. So they decided to start crèches where the women could leave the children when they went out to the fields to work.

At first, the crèches remained empty as the village women were prohibited from using them. It took many months and a lot of persuasion to get them to leave their babies in the crèches. The offer of food and care finally proved to be too tempting and some women defied their families and left the children in the crèches. Soon more mothers came in bringing their babies. When the mothers came back in the evening to pick their babies up, the crèche workers would talk to them about nutrition and health and everything else except the sensitive subject of *penn sissu kolai*.

Valli Annamalai says it took a couple of years for them to break through the barrier of silence. But, when the women finally began confiding in them, it was like opening the flood gates. Many women spoke openly about having killed their girl children. Some were unrepentant, others angry and many were filled with sorrow and guilt. What came through was the powerlessness of the women. Weeping angry women would argue with the social workers. 'What do you want us to do with our daughters?' they would cry. 'Why should we let them live? So that they can suffer like we do?'

Most women, however, were still afraid to even talk to 'outsiders' for fear of being beaten when they went home. The ICCW then tried recruiting local women to work at the crèches. Others were identified to monitor the 'high risk' mothers in each village.

In a bid to provide a viable alternative to killing, in the early 1990s, the ICCW introduced its own 'cradle baby scheme'. A few babies were left anonymously in the cradles. A couple of these babies also died. Was it neglect? Were they already weak babies? Or did their parents attempt to kill them before abandoning them? Anyway, the cradles became unpopular and the families reverted to their 'traditional' treatment.

So the social workers tried another approach. They asked them not to leave the babies anonymously in the cradle. The parents were encouraged to bring the babies in themselves. Or if they did not want to do so, they could send the baby with someone they knew. A person from the same village or the midwife usually brought the girl babies in. The parents were then given some time to take them back if they wanted to. More babies came in. Some took their babies back. Others gave them away for adoption.

This was the point at which the ICCW began insisting that if the parents wanted their daughter to be adopted, they had to hand in the baby themselves and get themselves sterilized. By 1991, they received a grant from the International Fund for Rural Development. Using this, they organized self-help groups in the SEWA model. Each group consisted of twenty women led by an animator and two elected members. These groups were taught to generate internal loans and later on encouraged to take external loans from banks. With this money they started some small income-generating activities of their own.

This encouraged the women to become more self-reliant. They learnt to create and handle assets. Women who had never stepped out of their villages before, learnt to go to banks and negotiate loans. They also learned to set up small businesses. One group of women for instance catered food for marriages. Another group provided chairs and furniture. Some even bought and cultivated land on their own. Once this programme got underway, the focus shifted to adolescent girls. Select groups of girls were taken to camps and workshops where they learnt about health and hygiene. They were also taught to take a stand against dowry and female infanticide. Gradually, adolescent boys were also targeted.

The arrest of Karupayee and the adverse publicity it generated, however, created another setback for the NGO, which had just begun to gain a foothold. Once more the villagers turned hostile and the men began prohibiting their women from talking to the social workers. ICCW now tried a multi-pronged approach.

Professional health care workers, doctors, psychiatrists, motivation specialists and others were roped in to give talks to the women. They introduced literacy classes, health camps and skill-training workshops. Although the women were often beaten up for attending the meetings, they began defying the men because they found the classes and workshops useful.

When I visited Usilampatti in 2005, I found that the number of infanticides in this area had come down to almost zero. I decided to go to some of the villages I had visited in 1994. A couple of the social workers who came with me had also accompanied me on my first visit.

At Alligundam, we had a totally different kind of reception. There was a wedding going on at one end of the village and a political meeting at the other end. The whole place wore a festive look with buntings and banners, and rival loudspeakers blaring out Tamil film music. But nothing else had changed. The same stream of dirty water ran through the main street which was still just a dirt road. The difference was in the reception we got. People greeted us with big smiles. They joked in a friendly manner with the social workers and invited us to attend the wedding. Was this the same village, I wondered, as we sat on rickety stools sipping tea at a tiny little shop at the village entrance.

The shop owner had given away one of his twin daughters for adoption ten years ago. He introduced me now to the daughter he had kept. Her education was now being sponsored by the ICCW. He sent her off to bring other 'saved' girls who were also getting sponsorships. The village animator brought another group of adolescent girls who were to attend a workshop the following week. It was a warm friendly group. No anger. No hostility.

Kanchamma, the midwife, had grown older but remained as physically and mentally alert as ever. She still lived in the same little mud hut and still delivered babies. We now sat and talked openly in the courtyard of a small temple near her house. The deities at the temple entrance towered over us ferociously as she posed for a photograph. Kanchamma seemed to have shrunk in the interim years but she was still as feisty as ever.

'I am fifty,' she said, when I asked her her age.

We laughed in disbelief.

'Okay okay. I am ninety,' she said. 'How does it matter how old I am? I still deliver babies. That is important isn't it?' She gave me a wide toothless smile. 'Things have changed now. I only deliver babies. No one wants to get rid of girl babies any more.'

But were there fewer girl babies being born now? She didn't have the answer to that question.

'Look at all these girls,' she said pointing to the girls in the crowd gathered around us. 'I have delivered most of them. And right here in their huts at home. Of course, many go to the hospital these days. It is easy. Not like before. Nowadays we don't even know which woman in the village is pregnant; or whether she delivered a son or a daughter.'

The group of villagers standing around nodded their heads and chattered in agreement. 'She is upset because she is going out of business,' one saucy young girl shouted. Her mother swatted her into silence.

In the other villages I was introduced to 'saved' girls, to 'reformed' mothers and families with just girls. I met Savitri who had killed two daughters before she was persuaded to keep her fourth one. Her elder daughter now aged fifteen had given up school and was working in the fields. The younger one just six years old was getting a sponsorship. Savitri had also been given a cow as an incentive and she was eking out a living selling milk. Her main worry however was about her two daughters. How would she get them married? She had no son for support and her husband was a wastrel. The cow and the sponsorship solved only some of her problems.

As we drove from village to village, the driver of the jeep, who was a local boy, talked about his childhood when he had seen so many baby girls disappear. Now things were different he said. Yes, they did seem different. Outwardly at least. But was it really so? Or was it all an illusion?

The doubts began to creep in as I sat in on the meeting of a local self-help group. The women were in a boisterous mood. They spoke about the confidence they had gained and the ways in which they were using the money they generated. One of the women who had just fixed her daughter's marriage said she had some financial problems as she needed money to pay the *varadatchinai*. So, was dowry still prevalent?

Of course it was! Which man would marry without dowry they asked. Mothers of sons too reluctantly admitted they had taken some 'token' dowry as they would otherwise be looked down upon. And the custom of giving *seer varasai* was thriving too. One woman even spoke of her friend who had taken a loan from her self-help group to pay for her daughter's wedding.

So how valuable was this new-found independence? If women were still the main commodities in a marriage transaction, how could their value as human beings have improved?

I found some answers to these questions at the SIRD office in Madurai. There I met Phavalam who was running the Campaign Against Sex Selective Abortions (CASSA). She was convinced that girl babies were still being eliminated. Only now it happened at a much earlier stage. Thanks to the easy availability of the scan which had penetrated deep into the villages, girls could be identified and eliminated while they were still in the womb, she said. The scan had become so cheap and easily available that women even from interior villages could find out the sex of their child and have an abortion. Killing a baby after it was born might generate a sense of guilt and invite punishment, but aborting a child in the womb was an unseen and comparatively safe act.

SIRD had conducted a five-year survey to understand the consequences of arresting and convicting families suspected of having killed their girl babies. They surveyed thirty families stretching across the 'infanticide belt' and found that in most of the areas, registering cases and punishing families had had no impact. In fact, even in the year 2000, some of the families they surveyed did not know that killing an infant girl was a serious crime.

On the other hand, the negative impact of the arrest on the families was quite devastating. Many of the women tried to commit suicide. Others were further pushed into poverty. Families broke up, and often it was the women who bore the brunt.

Take the case of Dhamayanti and Manickam of Salem. Manickam, a lorry driver, married Dhamayanti when she was seventeen. They had a daughter and a son. But Manickam wanted several sons. When their third child turned out to be a girl, his sister said she would bring bad luck to the family and fed her with salt water on the ninth day. The child died. A health worker who visited Dhamayanti on the tenth day found the baby girl missing and filed a complaint.

The whole family including Manickam's father was arrested under Section 302 of the IPC. They were later released on bail. None of them had realized the seriousness of the crime they had committed. Since many others in the family had eliminated girl children in the same way, they almost felt it was the natural thing to do. In fact, after his release, Manickam began pressurizing Dhamayanti to give him more sons.

Similarly, when Sumathi, an eighteen-year-old illiterate girl from Salem gave birth to a daughter in the Salem Government Hospital, her husband Muthu, a casual labourer convinced her that the baby had to be killed. Sumathi was Muthu's second wife. He already had a daughter by his first wife whom he had abandoned. Afraid that he might use his daughter as an excuse and abandon her too, Sumathi agreed. Muthu fed the baby poisoned milk and cremated the tiny body to get rid of the evidence.

However, Sumathi's parents who were working as casual labourers in Bangalore returned and urged her to book a complaint against Muthu for killing the baby. Sumathi went to the nearest police station and Muthu was imprisoned for thirty days under section 302 of the IPC. He faced the death penalty. A distraught Sumathi tried to commit suicide. She hadn't realized the consequences of any of her actions. Finally, Muthu was released on bail and the couple moved from Salem. Sumathi had one more daughter whom she was now bringing up with care. But she had not been able to live down her reputation as a woman who almost got her husband killed.

At the end of the five-year survey, the SIRD team concluded that mothers who were jailed faced a variety of problems. To begin with they were jailed when they were very weak after delivery and obviously in the jail they would not get the care which is normally given to a woman post delivery. The fragile psychological state of such women who would sometimes be facing postnatal depression was also not taken into consideration. Often, unconnected people were arrested and whole families ended up in jail leaving no adults to take care of the children. Since they were all arrested under

IPC 302, they faced life imprisonment or the death sentence. They also faced social ostracism as people who had gone to jail. Such a severe sentence, it was feared, would not act as a deterrent but would rather make families opt for the safer way out—namely sex selective abortion.

In an article on female infanticide in Tamil Nadu, Phavalam has said, 'SIRD analysed the complex aspect of the role of women in female infanticide and found that they actually inflict violence on themselves . . . women are trained to believe that their value is attached to the men in their lives. They are often socially ostracized if they displease or disobey their men and thus are encouraged to blame themselves as inadequate and incapable. This socialization process is reinforced by a culture where a woman's productivity is constantly devalued, her sexuality commodified, her work and character negated.'[1]

Phavalam feels that finally the woman internalizes this gender bias in favour of male children and kills her own female children in secret, even at the cost of endangering her own mental and physical health. In a way it is a kind of self-destructive act.

'Intense family and social pressures drive the woman to put an end to the life she has nurtured in her womb,' she says. 'The mother should not be punished for the crime and should be treated with sympathy and compassion. Charging the mother with homicide is double punishment for a victim of extreme gender discrimination.'

The SIRD study found that sexual violence was the root cause behind the massacre of girl children. A woman who gave birth to girls had no value in her own home. If she produced too many she could be thrown out of her marital home. Her birth family too would reject her. Killing her own daughters, therefore, was an act of self-preservation. If she defied society and kept them alive, she would probably end up alone with the additional burden of bringing up her daughters all by herself.

Viewed from a disempowered woman's perspective, the laws and judicial rulings make no sense. There may be a law against dowry, yet dowry demands just keep spiralling upwards. Killing girl children either before or after they are born is also illegal. So is violence against women. But, within the four walls of a home who is to enforce these laws? And if a woman does complain against her family, who is to support her for the rest of her living days?

At a public hearing on female infanticide, held in July 2002 by the Tamil Nadu State Women's Commission (SWC), activists felt that treating infanticide as homicide and booking the mother under Section 302 of the Indian Penal Code (IPC) for committing murder was excessively harsh.

The members of the SWC jury while commenting on a particular case said that infanticide was an inexcusable crime. 'The first task before us,' they said 'is to see that the baby girl is assured of her right to be born. If the deterrent aspect of the criminal law of homicide is removed or relaxed then the baby girl can, by no means, be ensured of her right to live. This is not a moment when the state can soften its instruments of crime prevention.'

However, the jury was also of the opinion that the mother of the infant should not be charged under Section 302 and should be given a milder punishment under appropriate provisions. They noted that 'The hand that takes the life of the infant may be hers, but the will is not.'

In fact, by the year 2005, many of the old schemes were being questioned. Activists felt, for instance, that having cradles and collection centres for girls only reinforced the stereotype of the unwanted girl child. Even parents who might otherwise have kept their baby were sometimes tempted to discard her because of the easy option they were offered. The thrust of all programmes they felt should be to motivate the parents to value the girl child and not to discard her. Activist groups like CASSA in fact felt that because of a wrong approach, the entire issue had just gone underground. Sex determination scans followed by gender selective abortions had replaced infanticide as a 'safer' option.

Tamil Nadu had launched a Protection Scheme for the Girl Child in 1992. The goal of this scheme, which was executed mainly through NGOs, was to eliminate female infanticide by the year 2000. Under its provisions, a poor family with one or two girls and no sons would be eligible for monetary incentives if one parent agreed to be sterilized. Money given in the name of the infant girl would be held in a fixed deposit account until she became twenty-one years old. Moreover, when the girl went to school, the family would receive grants for educational expenses. This scheme was intended to cover 20,000 families every year. In Salem district, in 1992, 614 girls received this benefit for about one and a half years.

Why did more families not benefit from these schemes? Apparently some of the NGOs in charge of distributing the funds cashed in on the helplessness of the beneficiaries who sometimes paid back half the money they received as bribes. Others, who were very poor and illiterate, were either not aware of the schemes or did not have the means to produce all the required certificates.

Writing about the limitations of such interventions, researcher and activist Sabu Geroge welcomed the idea of the state providing financial incentives for the education of girls. But, he felt that money made available for the girl when she reached the marriageable age of 21, would only help to legitimize the illegal practice of dowry. He also felt that since financial resources were limited, such social interventions would only cover a small segment of the needy population.[2]

Since most NGOs functioned with limited resources they usually could not have any long term strategy. They could only try to prevent individual cases of infanticide.

However, Sabu George pointed out that prevention of individual cases could not address the basic causes of women's subordination in society. Nor could it touch 'the large segments of the community who, although not directly involved in killing babies, are nevertheless guilty of abetting the perpetuation of the practice in silence.' He was therefore skeptical about 'the likelihood of such strategies bringing about any lasting changes in societal attitudes towards girls'.

Preventing individual cases of infanticide was also not easy. For instance, when a social worker found that a family was bent upon disposing of its female children, she could threaten to report them to the police. However, this could be a double-edged sword. If the family was arrested, everyone suffered, including the surviving children. The social worker might also experience a backlash from the community.

Of course, there was always the bribe factor. Policemen were often accused of taking bribes from families who did not want a case registered against them. In fact, in 1994, on my first visit to Usilampatti, I learnt that since many of the policemen belonged to the local communities that practiced infanticide, they were themselves guilty of killing their own female children. Hence, they were often hand-in-glove with the persons against whom cases were sought to be registered. The arrest of Karupayee took place because the policeman responsible was an 'outsider' who was appalled by the act.

On subsequent visits, I learnt of the dubious role played by the police at every stage. Policemen often accepted bribes from families to cover up cases of infanticide. They also threatened families with prosecution if they did not pay up. In fact, Sabu George has said in an article that health officials in Salem told him that the local police had asked them for a list of all female births so that 'they could visit the families and seek due favours.'

Thus in 2005, when the rest of the country was agonizing about the more widespread and 'technologically advanced' crime of sex selective abortion, Tamil Nadu's 'infanticide belt' continued to remain in the grip of the medieval practice of killing newborn female infants. During my last visit to Usilampatti, just as I was beginning to think infanticide no longer happened, I read of a mother and daughter who were trying to bury the body of a newborn infant girl on the banks of the Vaigai river in Madurai. The baby girl had been strangled to death.

But, as Lakshmi had asked me ten years ago, in what way was one method of killing better than the other?

3

Our Missing Girls

The map of Punjab looked as if it had been dipped in blood. It was October 2005. I was looking at this map in a booklet called *Missing: Mapping the Adverse Child Sex Ratio in India*. Radhika Kaul Batra, senior advocacy officer at the United Nations Population Fund (UNFPA) had given me this just released booklet. It gave a very graphic view of the deteriorating Child Sex Ratio (CSR) across the country.

The CSR is calculated as the number of girls per 1000 boys in the 0–6 age group. Since more boys than girls are born the world over under normal circumstances, there should normally be 950 girls to every 1000 boys in the below 6 age group. Anything below this indicates some kind of anti-female intervention. That is just a genteel way of saying they are being killed either before or soon after they are born.

The places which had a CSR of below 800 were marked in red on this map. Those with a CSR between 800 and 849 were marked in orange and those between 850 to 899 were marked in yellow. Areas with better ratios were marked in shades of green.

I looked at the 1991 map. There was no red or even orange on the entire map of India. Even in 1991, the whole of Punjab was yellow. In the 2001 map, all of Punjab was either red or orange. Not a trace of yellow. And the colour was spreading.

The whole of north India was turning from yellow and green to red and orange. It was very graphic. Girl babies were dying in hundreds.

These maps had been prepared using data from the 1991 and 2001 census. Maybe, by 2011 there would be no trace of orange it would be just red. Maybe by 2021, parts of the map would have black holes to show where women had been eliminated altogether.

It was a chilling thought. I turned to the last page. There was a map which showed the rate of decline in the CSR across the country over ten years. Red indicated the parts where the decline was more than 50 points. The northern and western parts of the country were covered with red splotches. Girls had disappeared from here with an astonishing rapidity. Delhi stood out like an ugly red pimple. India's girls were going missing at an alarmingly fast rate, and we don't even know about it. In fact, we don't even want to know about it. Like the man in the Usilampatti General Hospital, we produce our token girl children and say, 'She is a girl isn't she? Then where's the problem?'

It was ten years since I had made that visit to Usilampatti. Ten years since Karupayee was arrested. Girls were still going missing and at a much, much faster rate than before.

But, who were these missing girls? To whom did they belong? Obviously they could not all belong to poor, uneducated families like the ones I met in Usilampatti and Salem. More importantly, how did we know that so many girls had gone missing?

Noted economist Amartya Sen was the one who coined the term 'missing women'. His method of quantifying these missing women was quite simple and dramatic. Way back in the mid-1980s, when he found a gender skew in the sex ratios of several countries in South Asia, he used the tools of economics to understand this phenomenon. He compared the actual number of women in the countries where there was a skew to the actual number of women in some other countries. He found that the skew existed in countries which had a strong 'son preference'.[1]

Under natural circumstances the sex ratio at birth is around 940-950 girls per 1000 boys. However, given equal care, girls survive better than boys and so, the sex ratio usually evens out to about 1005 girls to 1000 boys. This ratio remains more or less the same through the next few decades of their life time. In fact, given equal treatment, women are generally better survivors than men.

To establish a benchmark, Sen took the ratio of women to men in sub-Saharan Africa as the standard. He chose this region because there was relatively little bias against women in terms of health care, social status and mortality rates even though the region did not come under the developed category. He found there were 102 women to every 100 men. In comparison, India had just 93 women to 100 men. So, using 102 women to 100 men as the benchmark ratio, Sen calculated that in India for every 100 men, there were 9 women missing.

'We can estimate the number of "missing women" in a country, say, China or India,' he said, 'by calculating the number of extra women who would have been in China or India if these countries had the same ratio of women to men as obtained in areas of the world in which they receive similar care.'[2]

Using this method, Sen calculated that in India alone there were 37 million 'missing' women already in 1986 when he first did the estimation. He said then, 'Using the same sub-Saharan standard, China had 44 million missing women, and it was evident that for the world as a whole the magnitude of shortfall easily exceeded 100 million.'

Amartya Sen ranked this among the worst human catastrophes of the twentieth century. Two other economists Klasen and Wink noted that this number of missing people was larger than all the people who died during the combined famines in the twentieth century, and the death toll of World War I and II combined. According to the World Bank, in demographic terms, a 100 million missing women represented 70 per cent of the current female population in the United States.

Was this being over-dramatic? Maybe. But it certainly was a good way of understanding numbers which otherwise look meaningless to the uninitiated.

Almost all the missing women belong to Asian countries where there is a long history of 'son preference'. In fact, India has historically had a deficit of women compared to most other countries. For instance, even in 1901 there were just 972 women to 1000 men. Subsequent census figures indicated that the number had been gradually decreasing until it reached an all-time low of 927 in 1991 and then rose again marginally to 933 in 2001.

To understand the enormity of the problem, one has to bear in mind that the population of India is around one billion. So if there is a shortfall of 70 women to every 1,000 men that means by 2001, about 70 million women had gone missing in India alone.

How did this happen? Could the census figures be wrong? Could it be that women were never counted when the enumerators came around? In parts of India, women are so devalued that only sons are mentioned as children. The girls become invisible people. They might not even figure in the census data. But how many women could have disappeared this way? Obviously they would represent just a small percentage of the missing women. So, what happened to the rest of them?

Were they killed as soon as they were born? Were their births never registered or even officially acknowledged? Had they died because they were starved or neglected by their own parents? Had they died because they did not receive proper medical attention while giving birth? Or had they died while having abortions under unhygienic conditions? Had they been brutally done to death by their own families because they failed to bring in dowry? Or killed because they were disobedient?

They might have died for any of a thousand reasons. But until the 1980s, they usually died after they were born. Not while they were still in the womb.

By 2001, an alarming and radical change had taken place. A careful analysis of the census data showed that over the decade, while the adult sex ratios in India had improved marginally, the child sex ratio had plummeted. Or, to put it simply, more women were staying alive, but fewer girls were being born.

In other words the skew in the sex ratio had acquired an extra spiral. Previously the sex ratio was bad because women and girls were dying of neglect, or because they were killed in a variety of ways after they were born. But now, they were not even being born. The most gruesome indicator of this was the plummeting child sex ratio.

In 1991, in India, there were 945 girls to every 1000 boys. This was close to the benchmark figure. However, by 2001, this number had fallen to an abysmal 927. Since the child sex ratio does not normally dip so rapidly and over so short a period of time it was obvious that something was amiss. Strangely, this was happening just at a time when female child mortality in our country was in fact declining at a faster rate than male child mortality. And this was worrying.

More baby girls were surviving now. This should have actually resulted in, at least, a slight improvement in the child sex ratio and not a decline. So, although the 2001 census figures had brought good news and bad news, the bad news had more far-reaching consequences than the good news.

The good news was that the rate of growth of population had come down in India during the decade since census 1991. It was in fact the lowest inter-census growth rate over the past fifty years. The adult sex ratio had also improved marginally and the female child mortality rate had gone down. So more women were actually surviving.

The bad news was really bad. The child sex ratio for the entire country had plummeted drastically. There was not a single state in this vast country, where the child sex ratio had not gone down. What impact would this have on future generations? If women were not even born any more, could extinction be far behind?

Actually, the all India figure did not really reflect the grim ground reality. The situation on the ground, at least in some parts of the country, was much worse. In some of the worst-hit areas, the ratio had declined to less than 800 girls per 1000 boys. In Punjab, Haryana, Himachal Pradesh, Gujarat and Maharashtra, the CSR had plummeted by more than 50 points in ten short years.

In Gurdaspur in Punjab there were just 729 girls to 1000 boys. In Mehsana in Gujarat, the figure stood at 752, in Salem in Tamil Nadu it was 763, and in Ambala in Haryana 772. At the bottom end of the ladder was Shahjahanpur district of Uttar Pradesh with a CSR of 678. In such places the benchmark figure of 950 looked almost meaningless. In these places there was a shortfall of more than 200 girls to every 1000 boys.

Social scientists, demographers and others working in the field had watched this situation developing over a period of time. After the 1991 census they had rung the alarm bells for states like Punjab and Haryana. But probably, no one realized how much worse the situation would get over the next ten years. In 1991, there were no areas in India where there were less than 800 girls to 1,000 boys. But by 2001 four states fell in the below 800 category.

The most shocking situation was observed in the capital city of Delhi. Sophisticated Delhi with its large urban educated population was the city where most girls were going missing. Thousands of girls were going missing every year right under the noses of the most powerful politicians and bureaucrats in the country. The worst hit was south Delhi, home to the rich and elite and presumably most educated.

South-west Delhi, one of the largest and most prosperous districts, recorded a drastic fall from 904 girls to 1000 boys in 1991 to 845 girls in 2001. Demographers calculated that 24,000 girls went missing in Delhi alone every year. News from the office of the Registrar of Births and Deaths was no better. Statisticians and doctors there monitoring the trend in Delhi confirmed that the situation had worsened in all the nine Delhi districts even since the 2001 census figures were published. The capital city in fact now ranked third after Haryana and Punjab among states having the lowest CSRs.

One more entrant into this category was Chandigarh, India's youngest city, planned by the famous French architect Le Corbusier in the 1950s. This brand new city was supposed to be a symbol of modern India. According to the 2001 census, in the rural areas around Chandigarh there were just 852 girls to every 1000 boys in 2001. Urban Chandigarh was worse with just 844 to 1000 boys.

However, the most shocking fact was that all over the

country, more girl children had disappeared from educated affluent urban areas, than from poor and illiterate rural areas.

In 1991, there were 948 girls to every 1000 boys in the rural areas. This was close to the benchmark figure. By 2001 this had come down to 934. The fall in the urban CSR was by far worse. It had come down from 935 girls to 1000 boys to just 903 girls to 1000 boys. A fall of 32 points in just one decade. The decline in the CSR in the urban areas of the country was, in fact, more than two times the decline seen in the rural areas. This decline was a particularly steep 83 points in Punjab followed by Chandigarh, Haryana and Uttaranchal.

Over a decade the situation had gone from alarming to terrifying. In comparison to the holocaust that seemed to be taking place, all other forms of violence against women, including infanticide, paled. The systematic elimination of women before they could even enter the world seemed to be a pan-national phenomenon.

The only faint silver lining was provided by the five states of Sikkim, Mizoram, Lakshadweep, Andaman and Nicobar Islands and Kerala, where the CSR showed improvements in the rural areas. Of these, Kerala was traditionally a women surplus state and the others were all either hilly or tribal lands or remote islands. In general, even though the numbers had dropped in all the states, the ones to the south and east of India had better CSRs.

In a way, there was nothing new about this trend. Certain regions of our vast and diverse society historically have had a stronger and more virulent preference for sons. Punjab, Haryana and Rajasthan for example have always had a deficit of women. Certain villages in Rajasthan have, in fact, not had a single female birth in decades according to old Government records.

Just as we were digesting all the bad news from the 2001

census, *The Lancet* came out with a startling article written by two researchers, Prabhat Jha of St Michael's Hospital at the University of Toronto, Canada, and Rajesh Kumar of the Postgraduate Institute of Medical Research in Chandigarh. They had collected data from a national survey conducted among 1.1 million households in 1998. Their findings were both distressing and shocking.

Around 10 million female foetuses may have been aborted in India over the past two decades, they said, because of ultrasound scanning and a traditional preference for boys. This kind of pre-selection, they said, had caused the loss of about 50,000 female foetuses every year. Based on the natural sex ratio in other countries, around 13.6 to 13.8 million girls should have been born in India in 1997. But actually just 13.1 million of them emerged from their mothers' wombs. On the fiftieth anniversary year of her independence, half-a-million girls had been denied the right even to be born in a country which prided itself on being the largest democracy in the world.

Amartya Sen had calculated the number of missing women. The 2001 census had given data on the number of missing girls. And now we had information on the number of girls who died before they were born.

The Indian Medical Association (IMA) disagreed with this number. A spokesperson acknowledged that prenatal selections used to take place, but said they were not as widespread as before and that *The Lancet* report was exaggerated. The IMA representative felt that pre-birth gender checks had waned since a Supreme Court crackdown in 2001.

Exaggerated or not, numbers help us to get a fix on the enormity of the problem. However, the much more worrying issue is the mindset which created the problem in the first place.

When did it all begin? And why?

Did parts of the country like Punjab and Rajasthan, which were always subject to invasion finish off their women in order to 'protect' them? Then how do you account for Kerala on the southernmost tip of India where some of the very first foreigners landed?

In Kerala, the Nairs who were soldiers led dangerous, nomadic lives. But they evolved a unique and peaceful system for protecting their women. They created the matrilineal *tharavadu* (joint family homes). The women stayed in their natal homes and property was passed on from mother to daughter. The Nairs did not kill their women to protect them. Instead, they created a safe environment in which their women could live.

However, in other parts of the country, killing women to protect them was a kind of tradition. Over generations, it had become so internalized that it was now almost like a mutated gene, passed on from mother to daughter and father to son.

In the early nineteenth century, the British declared some areas as infanticide prone. In 1805 they had found a high incidence of female infanticide among the Jadeja Rajputs of Saurashtra. In eastern Uttar Pradesh, there was a village with no daughters. In 1808, Alexander Walker, the chief authority in Baroda summoned the heads of all the communities and asked them to give an undertaking that they would not kill girl babies.

In 1870, the British government enacted the Prevention of Murder of Female Infants Act. To begin with, it was to be enforced only in the northwestern provinces including Punjab and Oudh. In 1872, some areas were notified as infanticide prone after census figures indicated a 40 per cent deficit of women. Already the women-killer belt was getting established. It stretched right across the north of India from what is now known as Gujarat in the west across Rajasthan and Punjab right up to present day Uttar Pradesh, Orissa and Bihar in the east.

In 1898, female infanticide was recognized as a crime and a government order was passed making it a cognizable offence. However, within eight years, in 1906, the Prevention of Female Infanticide Act was repealed as the government claimed that infanticide was no longer practised in these areas. The 1901 census actually indicated that there were just 832 females to 1000 males in Punjab. So, obviously the Act was withdrawn because of some other political considerations.

When societies kill their women, perhaps it is some primitive instinct at work. From the very beginning of civilization, anthropologists say, the supply of food has been a constant check on human population growth. Thus when food was in short supply, women and children were the first to be eliminated.

Darwin believed that infanticide, 'especially of female infants', was the most important restraint on the proliferation of early man. Sadly, over a period of time women continued to be killed at birth not because their death was necessary for the survival of the community, but because they were considered to be burdens in male-dominated societies.

In his book *Death by Government*,[3] R.J. Rummel, Professor Emeritus of Political Science, University of Hawaii, says that 'In many cultures, governments permitted, if not encouraged, the killing of handicapped or female infants or otherwise unwanted children. In the Greece of 200 BC, for example, the murder of female infants was so common that among 6000 families living in Delphi no more than one per cent had two daughters. Among 79 families ... there were only 28 daughters to 118 sons.'

He also says that in India, when demographic statistics

were first collected in the nineteenth century, it was discovered that in 'some villages, no girl babies were found at all; in a total of thirty others, there were 343 boys to 54 girls . . . in Bombay, the number of girls alive in 1834 was 603.'

Why did this happen? Were women always so unwanted in a country which is supposed to revere them? Does the rejection of female infants date back to Vedic times? A much quoted traditional blessing from the Atharva Veda states 'Let a female child be born somewhere else. Here, let a male child be born'. The son always had a positive role to play. He was equated to wealth and to blessings. His was the hand which strengthened the father in his old age. His was the hand which lit the funeral pyre that would send his father to heaven. The son or putra was supposed to liberate his father from hell or puta.

So important was it to have a son that the lawgiver Manu even made a provision for a son-less man to turn his daughter into an 'appointed' daughter or honorary son. According to this law, 'He who has no son may make his daughter in the following manner an appointed daughter (putrika), saying to her husband, "The (male) child, born of her, shall perform my funeral rites".' What if she had no male child? The law was clear on that too. 'But if an appointed daughter by accident dies without (leaving) a son, the husband of the appointed daughter may, without hesitation, take that estate.'

The woman on the other hand was viewed only as a bearer of sons. She was the 'field' in which a man would sow his seed to bear sons. Manu declared that 'day and night women must be kept in dependence by the males in their families'. A woman was always supposed to be dependent. 'Her father,' Manu declared, 'protects her in childhood, her husband protects her in youth, and her sons protect her in old age; a woman is never fit for independence.'

A double whammy. First women were declared to be creatures not capable of being independent, then they were labelled as burdens. Obviously the base line for behaviour was set by all these rituals and rulings, which clearly reinforced the idea that women were the property of men. They were burdens in need of constant vigil and protection. A daughter might be necessary to light a lamp in the house. A woman was necessary for procreation. But all women were, nevertheless, the property of their male relatives. They had to be guarded against defilement and it was the duty of the men to see that the wrong seeds were not implanted in them.

Over generations had both men and women so totally internalized these ideas that they could find nothing wrong in plucking out an unwanted female child from the womb as if it were some intrusive weed? The very fact that different parts of India have their own special traditional ritualistic methods for disposing of their unwanted female children indicates that 'son preference' is very deep rooted and goes a long, long way back.

History as well as mythology abounds with stories of great kings who performed enormous sacrifices and underwent rigorous penance in order to produce male heirs. Prominent among these is King Dasaratha, father of Rama who obtained a special payasam (sweet pudding) and fed it to his three wives who promptly gave him four sturdy sons.

At Tirupullani, ten kilometres from Ramanathapuram on the southernmost tip of India, the magical payasam is still given to childless couples. Tirupullani is a Vaishnavite temple whose antiquity is authenticated in the songs of the Alwars, the poet-saints of Tamil Nadu, who lived between the seventh and ninth centuries. It is a large temple with a kind of mysterious grandeur about it. Thousands of childless couples do *nagaprathishta* (installing statues of the snake god) at the peepul grove where Vishnu in the form of Adi Jagannatha had revealed to a rishi that he would be born as Rama. After installing the statues, the couples flock to the temple to partake of the payasam which is believed to have the same magical properties as the one which Rama's father, King Dasaratha, gave his barren wives. All of them pray that they will produce valorous sons like Rama and his brothers.

An interesting aside to this is the observation made by a well-known social worker in Chandigarh. 'I think Sita was one of the early 'saved' victims of infanticide,' she said to me. 'After all, she was found by King Janaka inside a pot buried in the earth.'

She was referring to the traditional method of female infanticide in this part of India. Here, she told me, the female infant was sealed alive inside a pot with a piece of jaggery and a bit of unspun cotton. She was then buried in the field while her elders stood around her and chanted, '*Ghur khaaveen, pooni katteen, aap na aveen, beere nu datteen.*' (Eat jaggery, spin yarn. You don't return. Send your brother.) It's a macabre thought, but totally plausible. Perhaps both Rama and Sita were products of some ancient form of sex selection!

When the Mughal king Akbar wanted a male heir, he made a pilgrimage to seek the blessings of the powerful sufi saint Sheikh Salim Chishti. His prayer was fulfilled, and soon, a son was born to him. In honour of the saint, Akbar named the prince Salim and built the magnificent city of Fatehpur Sikri to celebrate his birth.

Akbar, like Dasaratha was considered to be an enlightened king. The fact that they wanted male heirs to continue their lineage was not held against them. It was considered natural and appropriate that they should undertake pilgrimages and do penance in order to have sons who would rule their kingdoms and carry on the lineage. Every nook and corner of the country has places of religious worship, which cater to this deeply entrenched desire to have a son. In Bathinda in Punjab for example, people flocked to the Jandwale Baba, a pir, for granting a male child. Every Thursday, he held a darshan in his village, which was attended by people from far and near.

According to Rainuka Dagar of the Institute for Development and Communication in Chandigarh, this Baba had 'in his armoury' the rituals and practices of the three dominant religions of the region. Therefore, he attracted Sikhs, Hindus, as well as Muslims desiring sons. The Baba sometimes even recommended visits to medical practitioners. Perhaps Jeeda village, close to the Baba's residence, received the full force of his 'blessing'. By 2005, this village with an abysmal sex ratio was known as 'Kudimaar Pind' or 'Girl Killing Village'.

As Dagar pointed out, aspiring for a male child had the full support of society. The difference now was that people no longer had to rely on medicine men to fulfill their aspirations. 'People,' she said, 'no longer have to wait for the vagaries of God's blessings which like the monsoons are not controllable.' Science had come to their rescue.

4

Scientific Elimination

'What do you want?' the lady doctor asked. Her hand was on the telephone on the table in front of her.

My colleague Ammu Joseph and I were sitting in the small consultation room inside this doctor's nursing home in Krishnagiri in Tamil Nadu. The nurse in the ward outside had looked at us a little doubtfully when we told her we wanted to speak to the doctor. Obviously neither of us could be pregnant. Should we tell her we wanted to consult her about my fictitious, pregnant daughter-in-law? We had decided against that too. We looked too big-cityish and we doubted if she would believe us. After all, why would we come all the way down from Bangalore to Krishnagiri to consult this doctor?

It was the year 2001. Across the country sex selective abortion had played havoc with the child sex ratios. The Salem–Dharmapuri area, however, seemed to be caught in a time warp. Infanticide was still the norm as it was cheap, quick and decisive.

However, things were changing here too. Medical 'help' was now available to the women who could afford it. For a price they could now eliminate their girl babies even before they were born. It was neater and easier than infanticide. Besides, the chances of getting arrested were almost nil. A number of women in that area had told us about this doctor in Krishnagiri who had a special package for sex-selective scanning and abortion. One of the women, Padma, had even showed us her scan result with a tiny F scribbled in the corner. Her baby was saved because she could not afford the abortion and the village nurse had persuaded her to keep her third daughter, now four months old.

This gynaecologist, who had a flourishing practice, was married to a politically powerful person. She was also facing a court case filed against her by a man who had lost his wife during one such illegal procedure. We knew she wouldn't see us if we said we were journalists. Journalists and bureaucrats were responsible for most of her problems. Until they came into the picture, she had had quite a lucrative business going.

Speed was the key, we decided. So, before the nurse could quite decide what to do with us, we just pushed past her and barged in. The doctor was taken by surprise, but she politely asked us to sit down. We told her we were journalists investigating female infanticide in the area and since she had been practicing here for many years, we wanted to talk to her.

Her reaction to this was quite amazing. She picked up the phone on her desk and before we could say anything more, she quickly dialled a number. 'Some women who call themselves journalists want to talk to me,' she said to someone over the phone. 'Here, you talk to them yourself. I am giving her the phone.'

She held the receiver out to me. 'My husband would like to talk to you himself,' she said. 'He is in Delhi.'

Ammu and I looked at each other, taken aback. 'But we don't want to talk to him,' I protested. We could hear her husband's voice over the phone.

'We just wanted to ask you a few questions about the

women in this area,' Ammu said. 'We don't want to talk to your husband.'

The doctor just stared at us stony faced and held out the receiver.

'Hello, hello,' her husband was shouting over the phone. Obviously she was not planning to talk to us. I took the phone from her hand and placed it to my ear.

'What do you women think?' he was shouting. 'You think you can just pretend to be innocent and come in and ask all sorts of questions. What do you want?'

'Nothing,' I said. 'We didn't come here to talk to you. We wanted to talk to your wife.'

'You can't talk to her. You can only talk to me.' He was beginning to get abusive.

I put the receiver down on the table. Ammu picked up the visiting cards we had given the doctor and we left. As we walked out, we could hear her talking to her husband over the phone. She sounded very agitated. She had reason to. In 2001, sex selective abortion was illegal and if she was found guilty, she faced a jail term.

However, it was not always so. Once upon a time, not so long ago, doctors advertised their sex determination clinics with impunity. Sex selective abortion, in fact, was being touted as a kind of panacea for all social problems. In fact, at one point of time the use of medical technology for sex determination was being promoted as a tool for population control.

By the 1980s, it was becoming clear to demographers that the government's aggressive family planning campaigns of the sixties and seventies were beginning to backfire. People across the spectrum had by now realized the need to restrict their families. But they invariably felt that for a 'small family' to be a 'happy family', the children had to be boys. In that way they optimized their chances of 'happiness'.

So, how could they make sure they only produced sons? In the old days, it was a hit and miss affair. Those who yearned for sons would keep trying until they produced a couple of them. They would perform special rituals, visit specific temples, drink special potions and above all pray hard for a son. And sometimes they were 'lucky' and sometimes they were not.

Now, with a little technological help, they got 'lucky' all the time. Since aspiring to have a son always had the blessing of both religion and society, the transition from using traditional methods to scientific tools was smooth and untraumatic. According to the well-known demographer Ashish Bose, in India, there was 'an unholy alliance between tradition and technology'. Tradition, he said, was 'marked by son-preference'. When this was combined with technology which made sex determination easy, the combination was quite lethal.

'Today,' he said, 'ultrasound is the sex-selective technology that is widespread in most prosperous states. The reasons are easy to define—prosperity ensured better infrastructure, more machines and more doctors to perform the tests. People had money-power to pay for the technology and of course, as infrastructure improved, people could access the clinics easily.'[1]

The use of scientific technology for identifying the sex of the foetus was introduced to India in the mid-1970s. Dr Sabu George and Ranbir S. Dahiya have said in their article on female foeticide in Haryana, 'Indian medical researchers who pioneered amniocentesis in 1975 said it would assist those Indian women who keep on reproducing just to have a son, although this might not be acceptable to "persons in the West". Sadly, the doctors from the prestigious All India

Medical Sciences (AIIMS) in New Delhi were initially responsible for justifying the use of modern technology to identify male foetuses. In the *Indian Journal of Paediatrics* they claimed that the destruction of a few female foetuses would not affect child sex ratios and would actually free women from having to go through multiple unwanted pregnancies.'

How many girls went missing because of such medically encouraged foetal sex determination?

The numbers varied. Since there was no proper way of counting the number of sex selective abortions that could have taken place, all those who were watching the situation with growing concern could only make educated guesses.

According to Saheli, a Delhi-based NGO, nearly 78,000 female foetuses were aborted between 1978 and 1982. Over the next ten years, the number of sex determination clinics across the country multiplied. One survey estimated that between 1986 and 1987 about 50,000 female foetuses had been aborted. In the early days, the sex of the unborn baby was detected by using a process called amniocentesis.

Amniocentesis was first introduced in India in 1974 as part of a sample survey conducted by the AIIMS, New Delhi, to detect foetal abnormalities. It caught on like wildfire because right from the start, it was misused by doctors mostly to detect the sex of the baby in the womb.

For this test, a small quantity of the amniotic fluid is removed from the expectant mother's uterus and analysed for possible foetal abnormalities. It is done between the twelfth and sixteenth week of pregnancy and is completely painless. This test is performed only if it is absolutely necessary and if other tests point towards abnormalities in the child. There is always a tiny risk of miscarriage after this test. An area of skin on the front of the abdominal wall is treated with a local anaesthetic and a needle is gently introduced into the cavity of the uterus to withdraw a small quantity of fluid. The amniotic fluid reveals many important details about the foetus. A large number of congenital abnormalities can be detected, including Down's Syndrome and spina bifida, a congenital anomaly where the vertebral bones of the spine do not fuse.

What excited several Indian doctors the most was the fact that they could now tell the sex of the child by examining this fluid. The amniotic fluid was checked for the presence of a stainable spot called the Barr body in the nucleus of the cells. This spot was usually present only if the foetus was female. Another test, using a dye called quinacrine, looked for fluorescent bodies in the nucleus. The presence of these bodies indicated a male foetus. Very soon the medical profession had zeroed in on this important characteristic of the amniotic fluid as the most saleable.

In the early 1980s, Dr Sarala Rajajee, a paediatrician from Madras, wanted to spend a couple of months as an observer at a lab in the John Radcliffe Hospital in Oxford. The lab was doing research on the detection and diagnosis of ante-natal Thalassaemia through Amniocentesis and Chrionic Villus Sampling (CVS). This was an exciting new area of research in her field and she was looking forward to learning something new. However, when she went to meet the doctor in charge of the lab, she was shocked to find that he was very reluctant to let her in.

Says Dr Sarala, 'Dr Weatherhall told me that a number of Indian doctors had come and worked in the lab, learnt how to use these diagnostic tools and gone back home to use them only for sex determination.' Such a thought had never even occurred to her. She had a tough time convincing the doctor that her interest in these procedures was only for medical diagnosis.

In India, by then, amniocentesis as a tool for sex determination was already being used and flaunted as the latest technology in this field. India's first sex determination clinic opened in Amritsar in Punjab in 1979. It used amniocentesis to determine the sex of the unborn baby. Women's organizations across the country staged protests, but they were helpless as this new and revolutionary test was permitted by the Medical Termination of Pregnancy (MTP) Act because it was also used for detecting foetal abnormalities. So it could not be banned. There was no law which prevented the doctors from using the same equipment for determining the sex of the unborn baby.

A 1982 article on amniocentesis entitled 'Sex Determination Tests and Women's Health', in the *PUCL Bulletin* says, 'Amniocentesis is a procedure undertaken with certain definite indications for diagnosis of certain foetal conditions . . . [but] besides these specific conditions it is being used, or rather grossly misused, for doing antenatal sex determination (ASD). Knowing the implications of ASD in our present day society . . . it is totally unethical for any doctor to undertake such a procedure. But today we have doctors who are openly advertising clinics for just this purpose (ASD) in our leading newspapers.'

The article quotes from literature provided by the New Bhandari Hospital in Amritsar, which claimed to be doing the nation a service by 'keeping some check over the accelerating population as well as give relief to the couples requiring a male child.'

'Relief' mind you. Those who did not have a male child needed relief.

The advertisement literature also had some 'scientific' words of reassurance: 'Assessment of the sex of the foetus has been made possible by amniocentesis after completion of sixteenth week and up to twentieth week of pregnancy, when therapeutic abortion is medically feasible and legally permissible. The procedure involves withdrawing of amniotic fluid and transferring it to an autoclaved vial in aseptic conditions. This process has no side effects on the mother as well as on the unborn baby.' So, eliminating a female foetus was considered to be a 'therapeutic' abortion. The deformity obviously lay in the gender. The escape clause came much further down in the advertisement: 'In spite of all precautions, the procedures can be fraught with dangers of abortion in 0.1 per cent of cases only.'

The mortality rate however was much higher especially when the procedure was done by untrained people and under unhygienic conditions. The New Bhandari Hospital charged Rs 500 for doing the test. Since it was not registered to do an MTP, after the test the 'patients' were directed to a licensed clinic which did this procedure for Rs 600. So everything was above board and legal. The literature also claimed that the sex determination test was done only for women who already had one or more female children.

Soon more sex determination clinics came up. Their slogan: 'Pay Rs 500 now. Save Rs 50,000 later', became even more popular than the government's family planning slogan 'Hum do, hamare do.' (We two, our two.) The logic was if you paid the Rs 500 to eliminate your girl child you would save the Rs 50,000 which you would have to pay as her dowry later.

Women's groups and human rights activists protested. The Punjab government ordered the clinics to stop doing the tests for sex determination. Ironically, all the free publicity only generated more business. Since they were not doing anything illegal, the sex determination clinics cashed in on the publicity. At the New Bhandari Hospital the demand for these tests went up from one per day to four or five.

Since the test was conducted between the fourteenth to eighteenth week of pregnancy, and abortions were permitted up to the twentieth week, this was an issue that could not be contested. Besides, since the test was supposed to detect genetic abnormalities, the parents could claim they had aborted an abnormal child. A 1985 survey in Bombay revealed that 90 per cent of amniocentesis centres were involved in sex determination and nearly 96 per cent of the foetuses aborted were female. Since there was no law against it, all the government could do was issue circulars banning the misuse of medical technology for sex determination in all government institutions. This in turn led to the mushrooming of private clinics all over the country.

As early as 1976, the government had passed a partial ban against sex determination tests. In 1985, the Forum Against Sex Determination and Sex Pre-selection (FASDSP), a social action group in Mumbai, launched a campaign against sex determination clinics. In those early days, there were very few studies done on this new elimination technique.

In 1980, Ramanamma and Bambawali studied the records of three hospitals in Pune and found that between June 1976 and June 1977, 700 women had asked for sex determination in one of the hospitals. 95 per cent of the women who were told they would have a daughter went in for an abortion. On the other hand, 100 per cent of the women who were told they would have a son kept the baby even though they were warned that in some cases the child might have a genetic disorder.

In 1986, the Maharashtra state government appointed a committee to look into the issue. By then, sex determination tests were being done quite openly, but only by private practitioners. In 1986, there were an estimated 1000 gynaecologists in Bombay. About 70 per cent of them were private practitioners. According to an article in the *New Scientist*, in 1986 there were about 248 clinics and laboratories in Mumbai. Every year about 16,000 sex determination tests were being done in Mumbai alone. Between 1983 and 1986, about 75,000 female foetuses were aborted.

Sanjeev Kulkarni was asked by the government appointed committee to conduct a short sample study of prenatal sex determination tests and female foeticide in Mumbai city. The study covered fifty private gynaecologists chosen randomly from across the city and its suburbs.

The findings of this study were an eye opener. Most of the doctors said they did the tests only for determining the sex of the unborn baby and, in fact, they considered it a 'humane service' for women who wanted sons. Some of them, in fact, even said they suggested the test to their patients. Of the fifty doctors interviewed, forty-two said they used amniocentesis for sex determination. Between them, these forty-two doctors performed an average of 270 amniocentesis tests per month. Six of the forty-two doctors had now begun to use Chrionic Villus Sampling (CVS) as an alternative test for sex determination. In those days, the amniocentesis test cost around Rs 400 in Mumbai. CVS was more costly. Obviously doing these tests made good business sense.

Kulkarni found that public debate on the subject had only increased the demand for these tests. He also found that almost all the women who came for the tests belonged to the upper and middle classes. Maybe they were the ones who could afford the tests. Most of them already had a daughter or two. A few of them already had one or two sons and they wanted more. Doctors soon learnt to justify these sex determination tests as an effective tool for controlling India's burgeoning population.

The popular women's magazine *Eves Weekly*, which carried an article on sex selective abortion in 1982, quoted Dr S. Limaye, head of the Obstetrics and Gynaecology Department of the Bokaro General Hospital as saying, 'Our priority is population control by any means. Amniocentesis should be used as a method of family planning and made available to everyone at a minimum cost or even free.'

When Dr D.K. Tank took over as president of the Bombay Obstetrical & Gynaecological Society in 1986, he told the *Times of India*, 'Sex determination is a social problem like dowry and child marriage and there is no point in blaming the doctors alone by asking them to discipline themselves and refuse to do amniocentesis tests for those intending to abort a female foetus.' A Mumbai gynaecologist was positively ebullient. 'Emancipate the woman!' he cried. 'Make her important . . . I hope their number decreases so that their status in society enhances. After all, it is universal law that when demand escalates and supply dwindles, value automatically rises.'

As the years rolled by, more and more cash-happy medical practitioners pushed the theory that the status of the woman would increase as her tribe dwindled. The women flocked in greater numbers to the clinics, which promised them sons. Sex determination clinics had become the modern temples for the son-hungry.

In her book *Reproductive Rights and Wrongs: The Global Politics of Population Control* Betsy Hartmann pointed out that there was 'a very real danger that in countries like India, sex selection could become an established method of population control'. She quoted Dr D.N. Pai, a Harvard educated director of family planning in Mumbai who told the *New York Times* in 1976, 'If some excesses appear, don't blame me . . . You must consider it something like a war.

There could be a certain amount of misfiring out of enthusiasm. There has been pressure to show results. Whether you like it or not, there will be a few dead people.'

Almost twenty years later the Indian sex ratio was already showing an alarming skew. Yet, sex selection as a tool for population control still had its advocates. In 1994, a *New York Times* reporter blamed India's poverty on population growth and said that 'by pressing for the elimination of sex determination tests, women's groups are calling for curbs on a practice that has been one of few factors holding down a population increase.'

At the height of the battle, the activists fighting the tests were amazed by the unthinking remarks made, especially by the doctors. Social scientist Manisha Gupte, in a 1986 article, predicted that women would have to face major problems if the trend continued. 'With a highly adverse sex ratio,' she wrote, 'there is imminent danger that atrocities on women, including rape, purdah, forced polyandry and female infanticide will increase.'[3]

However, no one paid heed to such voices of warning. By the mid 1990s, confirming the sex of the child through 'scientific' means was a well-established and accepted practice.

The ultrasound scan for detecting genetic abnormalities in the foetus had come to India in the early 1980s. By the late eighties it had established itself firmly as a major tool for determining the sex of the unborn child.

In other parts of the world, ultrasonography as a diagnostic and therapeutic tool had contributed immensely to maternal–foetal medicine. Using the ultrasound machine, it was possible to obtain high resolution images of the foetal anatomy and to observe the various activities of the foetus while it was still in the uterus. But in India, the ultrasound scan was only seen as a kind of miracle machine that could determine the sex of the foetus at an early stage. The genitalia of the foetus is normally visible around the twelfth week. With the older scans, which had relatively low-resolution monitors, the sex could be determined only around the twentieth week.

However, scans now came in all sizes and degrees of technological advancements. The costlier trans-vaginal scans could enable the parents to find out the sex of their child within the fifteenth week, which meant abortions could be done earlier and hence would be safer. There were 3D colour scans and Doppler scans which helped doctors to visualize the foetus better. These were invaluable as diagnostic tools to doctors interested in foetal medicine. Though in lay terms it meant that even uninitiated parents would sometimes be able to recognize the sex of their child. Mobile sonography machines had become so sleek and compact that they could now be stowed away in the boot of a car. Even if a raid was conducted on a suspicious outfit, the chances were that the machine would not be located.

By 2000, the cost of sonography machines had come down. Major multinationals like Philips and GE, as well as local players like Wipro had got into the field and the machines were easily available in India. While this was a great boon for doctors actually interested in foetal medicine, it was a shot in the arm for those setting up sex determination clinics. Operating a sonography machine was also fairly simple. Studies conducted in various parts of the country revealed that quite a few scanning centres were actually owned and operated by non-trained personnel.

Dr Leela Visaria, Director of the Gujarat Institute of Development Research told me about the scanning centre she had seen in Bijnor in Uttar Pradesh in 2004. It was run by a transport services owner who had taken up this new 'business', more lucrative than his old one. Visaria said that he had set up shop inside one of his vehicles and advertised his sonography centre on one of his water lorries. He was doing brisk business, she said.

By the late 1990s, sex selective scanning had penetrated even the villages of Usilampatti. Asha Krishnakumar in an article in the fortnightly magazine *Frontline* dated 1998 describes her visit to some scanning centres around Usilampatti.

At noon on an unusually hot November day, the village street is deserted except for the occasional cyclist. In one particular building, however, there is a throng of people, most of them women, their numbers so large that they almost spill out on to the street. Here is an ultrasound scan centre which offers pre-natal diagnostic facilities, ostensibly to monitor the health of the foetus but, in many cases, to determine its sex for a deadly purpose.

Over by a corner, quite oblivious to the presence of others, Sarasamma, who has just had her foetus scanned, and her mother-in-law are arguing loudly, but in a chilling matter-of-fact tone, about when to snuff out a life: should the female foetus that Sarasamma bears be killed in the womb or should they wait a few months for the baby to be born and then starve her to death?

Going 'scientific' had become easy for the villagers as, for a small price, the information regarding the gender of their unborn babies was available right at their doorstep. They could now 'send off' their female children without going through the messy process of killing them after they were born.

According to Krishnakumar, in 1998 there were 'thirteen scan centres in and around Usilampatti taluk: three in the town, five in Theni, two at Thirumangalam, and one each at Andipatti, Vathalagundu and Kallupatti.' Madurai city, forty kilometres from Usilampatti town, had 'over a hundred scan centres'.

She also said that 'All the scan centres in Usilampatti taluk operate illegally—they have not obtained certification of registration from the appropriate authority as required under law. For Rs 150, the centres scan foetuses to determine the sex—in blatant violation of the law and medical ethics—and discreetly disclose the one bit of information that will decide whether or not the foetus will be allowed to live: its gender.'

A study on the functioning of Ultrasound Sonography Centres in Karnataka conducted by the Population Research Centre at the Institute of Social and Economic Change (ISEC), Bangalore, revealed that by the beginning of 2004, there were 1621 ultrasound sonography centres in Karnataka for which registration had been granted. Over 25 per cent of them had neither an owner nor an operator who was qualified to use the machine. Of course those in the field knew that the number of machines available for scanning was much higher. Although all those using the sonography machines were required by law to register their machines and to keep proper records, most of them did not. When caught they usually pleaded ignorance.

A study conducted by the Gokhale Institute of Politics and Economics in Maharashtra in 2004, established a clear correlation between the number of sonography centres and decline in child sex ratio. The average sex ratio for districts with more than 100 sonography centres was 901, and for districts with less than 100 sonography centres it was 937. A difference of 36 points. Maharashtra, the report said, had the dubious distinction of having the maximum number of sonography centres in the country. Most of them were privately owned and located in the wealthy urban and rural pockets of the state.

Even by the mid 1990s, it became obvious that sonographic scanning of the foetus for 'genetic abnormalities' had come to stay. And, in a son-hungry society like India, the female foetus had no hope. She was definitely considered genetically abnormal. By the year 2005, ultrasound scanning for sex detection had become a Rs 500 crore industry. And it was totally illegal.

5

Going Hi-tech and Global

The bumpy unpaved road wound its way leisurely through rich green fields. The light-purple heads of the sugar cane crop waved in the gentle wind. A rich aroma of jaggery wafted through the taxi window. The year was 2005 and I was driving to Pandavapura in Mandya district in Karnataka in south India.

Childhood memories came floating in. I remembered visits to the temple town of Melkote very close to Pandavapura. Every couple of miles, my father would stop at a wayside 'sugar cane factory' and we would pile out of our capacious Ambassador car to drink sugar cane juice fresh from the fields and gorge ourselves on the jaggery hot from the vats. We would sit on boulders holding in our palms the steaming jaggery piled on to banana leaves. As we nibbled at it, we would watch the oxen going round and round and inhale the fresh smell of the cane getting crushed in the pit. The friendly villagers would ply us with more juice and more jaggery. Everything was warm, comfortable, laid back ... and probably inefficient.

The aroma was irresistible. On an impulse, I asked my taxi driver to stop and went into the shed from which the delicious smell came. I was amazed—I had entered a totally different kind of factory.

Mountains of sugar cane were fed into huge machines. The juice was collected in bins and processed and sent into hi-tech vats. 'Sorry,' the supervisor said. 'We have no way of collecting the juice to give you a glass to drink.' As for the jaggery, it was all packed into bucket-shaped moulds and kept ready for dispatching to other parts of the country. I could only buy a cold bucket if I wanted to and that too only if the owner agreed.

The owner drew up in a big Qualis. 'Yes Madam, we have also gone global,' he said proudly. 'Our jaggery goes all over the country now. And even all over the world. Did you see our equipment? Everything is streamlined now. Very hygienic. Very efficient. Not like the old days.'

Very efficient. That was the problem. Everything was a little too efficient. Especially in some areas. Nothing was left to chance any more. Certainly not the sex of one's child. Mandya district now had one of the lowest child sex ratios in Karnataka. From a fairly healthy 950 girls to 1000 boys in 1991, it had dropped to 937 in 2001. Thirteen points in just ten years. And the indications were that the CSR was continuing to plummet downwards. In rural Mandya, it was already below 900.

Fertile Mandya district has always been prosperous. With new generations of young farmers taking over the helm that prosperity had taken on a new meaning. More money, more goods, bigger houses, bigger dowries . . . and the rest of the story was the usual one. Girls were no longer wanted in Mandya district.

I had spent the morning in Mandya town with Janardhan and Gowri, who worked with Vimochana, the Bangalore based NGO. There were twenty-nine scan centres in Mandya town alone, they told me. We drove through the town looking at them from the outside. Some were tucked away in quiet residential localities. Others lay in the busy heart of the town. Janardhan pointed out the house of a doctor couple who were allegedly doing scans and abortions in their private nursing homes. But nothing could be proved. The doctors in Mandya were too smart to get caught. When the Lok Ayukta conducted a raid, the nursing homes seemed to have got prior intimation. He could find no incriminating evidence. Their sting operations were also not successful. An NGO sent a pregnant colleague to some nursing homes to see if she could catch some of the doctors revealing the sex of the child on tape. Even that did not work out. The doctors had learnt to be wary.

Ever since scanning for sex determination had become illegal, the whole business had gone underground. Now everything was shrouded in secrecy. You needed 'recommendation', and all along the line, the agents had to be paid off.

In Bangalore, Donna Fernandes of Vimochana who was spearheading the drive against female foeticide in Mandya told me the issue was fraught with problems. Even when they managed to collect evidence against the scanning centres or against doctors, the health authorities who had the final say never booked any complaints. They were all hand-in-glove with each other, Donna said. Even when they sent decoys and successfully trapped doctors, the doctors managed to bribe their way out.

Pandavapura, the little town I was heading for, was in the heart of the cash-rich Mandya district. It was once known only for its laid back rusticity and its temple. Today, it was one of the areas where the sex ratio was declining at an alarming rate. I just wanted to take a look at its one and only nursing home. I knew I wouldn't be able to get anyone to talk as I had no contacts.

My taxi driver, who was from the nearby big city of Mysore, was curious. Why on earth did I want to visit this nursing home in the middle of nowhere? He didn't believe me when I told him that there was a shortage of girl babies in this district. They were all stories made up by the media, he said. Whenever they didn't have anything to write about they created some such 'scare'.

Janardhan, however, had a different take on this. He told me about the number of media persons who had come and gone away with no concrete evidence. He had gone with two television crews to some villages. All the villagers swore that they never discriminated against girls. Yet the child sex ratio continued to plummet.

Pandavapura, like Usilampatti was a rural area. However, the comparison ended there. The villagers of Usilampatti, who 'sent away' their baby girls after they were born, eked out a living on lands which often belonged to other people. The sugar cane farmers of Mandya who aborted their baby girls before they were born were rich and well educated.

As Lakshmi of Alligundam had asked me ten years ago, in which way was one form of killing worse than the other?

The nursing home in Pandavapura stood on a side street hedged in by houses. It was very busy. Women of various ages and sizes were walking in and out. There was a big board which said 'Scanning for sex determination is illegal'. The walls had a couple of framed pictures of chubby baby Krishnas.

I sat in the lobby watching families chatting, carrying baskets of food and dealing with bawling children. Everything looked so normal and comfortable. Was the taxi driver right? Was it all some media created myth?

No, my activist friends in Mandya town had assured me. Pandavapura was quite famous for its scanning facilities. They told me there was even a mobile sonography machine located in a church centre.

Of course in the year 2005, those who operated the scan centres no longer made the kind of mistake which got the doctor in Krishnagiri into trouble in the late 1990s. They made no marking on the scan results. In fact they didn't even openly say whether the foetus was male or female. They had learnt to be careful.

The gender identifiers had evolved their own specific 'area' codes linked to the tradition and jargon of the part of the country where they lived. In parts of north India, 'laddu' stood for son and 'barfi' for daughter. If the woman was asked to come back on Monday, it meant she was carrying a son. If she was asked to return on Friday, it meant the foetus was female and she would have to abort it. Some doctors gave a V sign. If a doctor frowned it meant the baby was female. If the doctor smiled and shook the patient's hand it meant all was well, it was a boy. Some doctors just gave a discreet thumbs-up sign to indicate it was a boy.

The couples who went in for sex selective abortions too had learnt to be careful. In Gujarat, Ila Pathak, director of the Ahmedabad Women's Action Group (AWAG), told me that couples went in for scanning and abortion in different places and under different names. It, therefore, became almost impossible to co-relate the two actions.

'In fact, as you probably know, sex selective abortion has gone international,' a doctor in Delhi told me. The year was 2005. We were sitting in her comfortable home talking about this phenomenon, which was spreading like an epidemic. The doctor, who obviously wished to remain anonymous, was quite knowledgeable. This was not surprising, as she had a clinic which was quite popular with NRI women wanting abortions.

'It has been carried by our NRIs across the seven seas,' she said. 'After all, our Indian families always carry with them all our traditions, good and bad. Wanting a son, as you know, is a well-entrenched and accepted Indian tradition.'

According to this doctor, son-hungry NRI families got the scan done in the US where revealing the sex of the child was legal. Then, if the foetus was of the 'wrong' gender, they returned to India and got a cheap and legal abortion done. Women from UK, on the other hand, came to India for the scan as many clinics in the UK refused to reveal the sex of the foetus. She had been dealing with such cases for a couple of years now. It was in fact quite a lucrative niche market.

Gynaecologist Puneet Bedi who had been tracking female foeticide across the globe said that the sex ratio at birth in the Indian community in New Jersey was as bad as Punjab and Haryana. He also said that there was anecdotal evidence pointing to some doctors of Indian origin who were referring patients to India for abortion of female foetuses.

Sex determination using ultrasound takes place only after twelve weeks. NRI women wanting to abort their female foetuses after that came to India where there were private clinics which specialized in this. Over the years, doctors in Indian clinics had become specialists in the medical procedure called partial-birth abortion. If the baby has to be aborted, for instance, after around twenty-four weeks in the womb or two-thirds of a full-term pregnancy, the foetus has to be pulled out from the mother feet first, up to the neck. The doctor then creates a hole in the skull with scissors to take out the brain, making it easier to collapse the head and pull it out completely. This gruesome procedure was banned in the UK when it was done for non-medical reasons.

It was banned in India too, but who cared?

In fact, even in the UK, in 2002, some NGOs had found

that private sex determination clinics in London, Birmingham and Glasgow were advertising in the Punjabi newspapers. In 2005, when Dr Sabu George spent some time in Leicester, he was told by the local Indian community leaders that British Asian women went to India for sex selective abortions because they were cheaper and easier there.

In January 2006, the British paper *The Observer* investigated the existence of female foeticide among British Asians. 'Abortion of female foetuses has long been a part of life in Britain,' the article said 'and *The Observer* has uncovered evidence that pregnant British Asian women, some in effect barred by the NHS after numerous abortions, are now coming to India for gender-defining ultrasounds and, if they are expecting girls, terminations.'

A report by the Commons Science and Technology Committee released in 2005 found that 'Some UK communities do have a decided preference for boys over girls.' And that the 'social need' for male children, particularly among Britons of Indian descent, was widespread.

The Observer reporter, Dan McDougall, tracked a couple of British Asian women who had come down from Leicester to have sex selective abortions in Delhi. They told him that because of the more stringent laws in Britain now, they could no longer find out the sex of the baby in Leicester. Besides, they would not get covered by the National Health Scheme (NHS) as they had already gone in for a couple of abortions to get rid of unwanted girl babies.

McDougall talked to Ritu, the twenty-seven-year-old mother of two girls from Leicester whom he found in the waiting room of the Kalkaji Family Planning Clinic in South Delhi. Ritu, who was just over fourteen weeks pregnant, told him, 'I'm here because we were already coming on holiday to see relatives. I had an ultrasound here a few days ago. It cost about £20 and we found out I was having a girl.' Her mother-in-law told her to abort the baby because 'the family wants a boy'. Ritu was forced to get it done in Delhi because she had already had sex selective abortions in the UK. Since the NHS was suspicious of women who had repeated abortions she knew she would not be able to get an affordable scan and abortion done in Leicester.

'Anyway, it is cheaper here,' she told McDougall. 'Only £100—and the doctors are excellent.'

McDougall also interviewed Dr Revati Mukundan at the clinic and she told him, 'We can abort at over twenty weeks pregnant and the delivery of the foetus at that stage is difficult. Certainly we can do it, but we would need to have specific grounds for the procedure, and I can assure you a complaint about the sex of the child is not a good reason. We have had a number of British clients, but also clients from the Middle East and Germany. We offer a professional and caring service.'

Ritu told him of her two aunts in Britain who had had five abortions between them in their quest for a boy. Both were eventually refused ultrasound tests in Leicester and had to have them done privately.

'There are clinics in Leicester,' she said, 'that won't identify the sex of babies to Asian women. They have a policy, they say, so more British Asians are coming to India when they are pregnant to make sure everything goes to plan.'

The doctor in Delhi was right. The epidemic had definitely crossed the Indian borders and spread worldwide.

Meanwhile, in the 2000s, more hi-tech gender determination tests were coming in. Almost all these tests had initially been designed to identify sex-related genetic diseases. Since abortion of an 'unviable' foetus is easier at an earlier stage, the tests which were faster and simpler were popular. These were sparking off ethical debates even in countries where there was no gender preference.

Pre-implantation genetic diagnosis for instance takes place even before a pregnancy begins. Doctors called it a cutting-edge screening test, which helped ensure that gender-related genetic problems were not passed on to the offspring of parents who carried a faulty gene. This could be misused not just for producing children of the desired sex, but also for creating 'designer' babies. Sex determination clinics, which used pre-implantation techniques had been advertising in the mainstream media in the US for years now.

In 2001, *India Abroad*, the magazine meant for Indian émigrés in the US carried a couple of ads for such clinics. The pitch was clear and focussed. They were aimed at the son-hungry Asian-American population. These clinics offered the latest hi-tech scientific processes so parents could pre-select the gender of their baby even before it was conceived. There was a sense of déjà vu. They almost sounded like the old Indian sex determination clinic ads. They reminded us that the now unpopular amniocentesis was once cutting edge technology for sex selection. And that was just twenty years ago.

'Desire a Son?' asked one ad. 'Choosing the sex of your baby: new scientific reality,' said another. One ad which ran in both in *India Abroad* and the North American edition of *The Indian Express* said 'Pregnant? Wanna know the gender of your baby right now?'

Obviously there was a market for these expensive sex selection tests among the Asian-American population. One of the doctors who advertised was Dr Andrew Y. Silverman, the medical director of gender-selection centres in Manhattan and White Plains. He told the *New York Times*, 'The ethnic groups that are moving in—from the Asian subcontinent and China—have a tradition of wanting boys. Just from my own patient population, I'm seeing an increase in those kinds of patients. That's why I started advertising in *India Abroad*.'

Dr Masood Khatamee, professor in the obstetrics and gynecology department at the New York University School of Medicine and the executive director of the Fertility Research Foundation said he decided to advertise in *India Abroad* because he had seen an increase in the number of Indian clients coming to him for gender selection or, as he put it, 'family balancing'.

It was so demoralizing. Technology had moved by leaps and bounds, but on the ground nothing had changed. If anything girls were more unwanted than ever. Following protests from women's groups both in India and the US, *India Abroad* decided to withdraw the ads and not to accept any more ads for sex selection clinics. At that point of time the magazine had a circulation of about 65,000 in the US and Canada.

'We all felt a little queasy,' said Ajit Balakrishnan, the chairman of Rediff.com India Ltd., which had bought the English-language newspaper just two months prior to the airing of the ads. 'We don't want to be remotely associated with anybody that discriminates for a boy child over a girl child. It's wrong to discriminate. You know, some years ago many of my friends marched through Delhi and Bombay to get the government to get rid of these tests.'

These clinics offered the very latest technology for sex selection: sperm separation. This was an expensive procedure and sometimes painful as well as harmful to the woman, especially when eggs had to be harvested for in vitro fertilization.

The cost for each insemination was $1000 to $1500, but neither Dr Silverman nor Dr Khatamee guaranteed that a woman would conceive. And, of those who did conceive, they said, about three out of four would achieve the desired results.

Since such gender-selection methods did not always give the hoped for results, probably only 'a desperate or especially determined woman may abort the foetus if it is not of the gender she wanted,' the doctors said.

Most of the clinics used a process perfected by Dr Ericsson in the 1980s. The sex of the baby is determined by the sperm which fertilizes the egg. The egg only has X chromosomes. The sperm can carry either an X or a Y chromosome. The baby would be a boy only if the egg was fertilized by a sperm carrying a Y chromosome. The Ericsson technique is based on the fact that sperm carrying the Y chromosomes move faster than the ones carrying the X chromosome.

Using a laboratory process, the sperm is passed through a sticky protein liquid, the assumption being that the slower moving X sperm would get stuck while the Y sperm would whiz through. The process is repeated till a concentrate of Y bearing sperm is collected. This concentrate is used by a doctor or even a qualified nurse to inseminate the eggs in the mother's uterus. Over the years, this process had been streamlined in the US. In 2003, Marcy Darnovsky, the Assistant Executive Director at the Centre for Genetics and Society expressed concern over the growing number of ads which propagated 'family balancing', a euphemism for sex selection.

'Several times over the past few months,' she wrote, 'a small but striking ad from a Virginia-based fertility clinic has appeared in the Sunday Styles section of the *New York Times*. Alongside a smiling baby, its boldface headline asks, "Do You Want To Choose the Gender Of Your Next Baby?"'

If so, the ad continues, you can join 'prospective parents . . . from all over the world' who come to the Genetics

& IVF Institute (GIVF) for an 'exclusive scientifically-based sperm sorting gender selection procedure.' The technique, known by the trademarked name MicroSort, is offered as a way to choose a girl or boy either for the 'prevention of genetic diseases' (selecting against the sex affected by an X-linked or Y-linked condition) or for 'family balancing'.

Darnovsky's concern was that the ads for 'hi-tech methods of sex-selection' were now going mainstream. The ads no longer bothered to even pretend they were marketing these techniques for anything other than 'social purposes'.

In 2001, a US company called Gen-Select ran a series of advertisements in the *Times of India* for a gender selection approach that was supposed to be safe and easy to use and 'up to 96 per cent effective'.

Gen-Select was not exactly cutting edge technology, but the promoters cushioned their product with a lot of pseudo-scientific jargon. The mother-to-be would be put on a diet of 'carefully formulated gender-specific nutriceutical supplement', they said. This included 'specific univalent and divalent cationic elements' which combined with specific vitamins and herbal extracts created 'the strongest bias possible for successfully accomplishing conception of the requested gender'. All the nutriceuticals were supposed to be produced in Food and Drug Administration approved facilities in the US.

Once the diet was established, then the woman's monthly ovulation cycles were to be monitored by recording changes in the body temperature with a thermometer provided along with the kit. The couple was advised to have sex either immediately before or after ovulation depending again on the 'requested' gender. The kit also came with sprays and douches which would alter the acidic or alkaline environment of the female reproductive tract. Y sperms they said survived better in an alkaline environment and X sperms in an acidic one. The kit was priced at about Rs 6000 and was touted as being safe and non-invasive. When journalists from the magazine *Frontline* contacted the promoters of this product, they claimed that their motive in selling it in India was not commercial but 'ethical'!

'We found that the people of India have a strong desire to choose the sex of their children and frequently go to the extreme of foeticide to achieve this goal,' the promoters said. 'With our product the freedom to choose the gender of your next child is preserved while the moral, ethical and legal issues of foeticide are put at ease.'

They also claimed that a part of the proceeds from the sale of every Gen-Select kit sold in India would be donated to the cause of the prevention of foeticide! They said that since their method of selection was pre-conceptional and not pre-natal, they were not breaking any law.

It was almost like the old days again. Women's groups staged protests against the *Times of India* for carrying the ad and the newspaper was forced to withdraw it.

The paper, however, took one last final stand and defended its original decision to run the ad. In an editorial entitled 'Sophie's Choice' the paper claimed it was upholding the woman's democratic right of 'freedom of choice'. Even while condemning the use of technology for gender selection and abortion, the *Times of India* editorial asked 'Can we abridge an individual's right to choose the gender of her child before conception?' However the incident had a positive fallout as well. The Pre-Natal Diagnostic Techniques (PNDT) Act was amended in 1993 to bring pre-conception gender selection techniques under its purview.

Ironically, over the years, in the process of developing new investigative procedures to monitor foetal health, medical scientists had unwittingly signed the death warrant of millions of unborn females. The process of interference could now definitely begin right before conception.

Another new technique, known as PGD or Preimplantation Genetic Diagnosis, originally developed to sort out human embryos with hereditary defects, had rapidly been adapted to select and eliminate female embryos. The doctors using this technique allowed the eggs to develop to an eight-cell stage after in-vitrio fertilization. Then one cell of each egg was analysed. Not for diseased genes but for the unwanted XX (female) chromosome.

In October, 1997, a London clinic announced its first success using this method of sex selection when a woman became pregnant with a boy, at a cost of $18,000. This technology was rapidly absorbed by the fertility clinics in India. By the year 2000, the same 'service' was made available at a cost of about Rs 8 lakhs. The users felt ethically quite smug as they had neither broken a law nor had they actually taken a life as they perceived it.

Since many of the new sex selection technologies were used before pregnancy, the debate had now entered an uncharted arena. Some countries like the UK decided to prohibit 'non-medical' sex selection. In 2003 their Human Fertilization and Embryology Authority recommended that sex selection for 'social' reasons should continue to be prohibited and that the authority's purview be expanded to include regulation of sperm sorting technologies as well as other sex selection procedures.

Meanwhile another avant-garde test entered the market in June 2005. The Baby Gender Mentor, allowed a woman to determine the sex of her baby by taking a home blood test just ten weeks after conception. This new test could peg gender eleven weeks earlier than the routine ultrasound. Besides, it could be done in the privacy of her own bedroom.

This blood test used technology which had been in trial for fourteen years. The Baby Gender Mentor Home DNA Gender Test employed what it called 'cutting-edge, patent-pending technology' to attain the earliest gender detection with what they claimed was 'unprecedented sensitivity and unsurpassed accuracy'. This technique traced the amount of Y chromosomal DNA in the maternal blood to determine gender.

New research had revealed some hitherto unknown information about foetal DNA. Until recently doctors thought that no trace of the just-conceived baby passed through the thick wall of the placenta during the first couple of months. However, it was now proved that during pregnancy, a variety of cell types of foetal origin, as well as foetal DNA, crossed the placenta and circulated within the mother's peripheral blood. This foetal material was a source of information about the gender as well as the genetic makeup of the developing foetus. Foetal genetic material could be detected in maternal blood very early in gestation.

The discovery of foetal DNA in maternal plasma and the demonstration of the relative ease and reliability with which it could be detected and harvested, had opened up new possibilities for non-invasive prenatal diagnosis. The greatest practical problem was to differentiate foetal DNA in maternal plasma from maternal DNA. Once this was solved, gender identification at a very early stage became easy.

The gender detectors examined the mother's blood plasma for Y chromosomes. The idea was simple. A girl baby's DNA would be indistinguishable from that of her mother because like her mother she would be carrying only X chromosomes. So, if the Y chromosome DNA was present in the maternal blood sample, the unborn baby would be a boy. Its absence meant the baby was a girl.

Reading about this test gave me an eerie feeling. Only the presence of a baby boy could be detected. It was almost as if the baby girl went into hiding because if she revealed herself she would be eliminated. The advertisement for this kit said 'Now there's a scientific, non-invasive way to predict your baby's gender—with 99.9 per cent accuracy. With a few drops of your maternal blood you can find out your baby's sex as early as five weeks after conception with the new Baby Gender Mentor Home DNA Gender Testing Kit'.

The kit gave three easy steps to complete the prenatal gender test. The mother had to ring a toll free number and talk to a 'counselor' who would send a 'collection kit' and arrange for her blood sample to be collected at a local hospital. The location of the hospital and time would be fixed by the promoters. She would then have to go with her kit and give the blood sample which would be packed into a prepaid envelope and posted to the lab. The results would then come to her via fax, email or phone within ten working days.

So frighteningy simple and easy.

In the US, this test was billed as a non-invasive one which gave 'curious parents the option of knowing the gender of their baby as early as ten weeks into gestation', by sampling only the mother's blood. They made no bones about it. The kit was meant for detecting the gender of the foetus for purely non-medical reasons. The test was not yet available in India. But the day was not far behind. By 2006, this kit known in local parlance as 'Jantar Mantar' was freely available and widely used in Punjab and Haryana. Even as we were wondering about this, there was one more breakthrough, which looked as if it would add a totally new dimension to this method of sex detection.

Researchers found they could achieve 100 per cent success

in detecting the presence of a male foetus even from dried maternal blood spots. This meant that maternal blood could be collected and transported from remote places for analysis. The ramifications of these new technologies are quite mind-boggling, especially when you realized that in the US, where most of them originated, sex selection technologies and marketing were largely unregulated.

The American Society of Reproductive Medicine (ASRM) had drawn a distinction between medically indicated sex selection to prevent X-linked genetic disorders and 'social' sex selection for reasons such as family balancing.

Though ASRM recommended against 'social' sex selection, there was no enforcement mechanism and no legal regulation of sex selection technologies in the US. The new technologies like sperm sorting and Pre-Genetic Diagnosis were perfectly legal. Kits like the Baby Gender Mentor did not even require licensing.

Past experience has shown us that we Indians are very quick to adopt such new technologies especially when they have commercial value. The booming sex selection industry is like an eager sponge just waiting to soak up the latest and quickest methods. With every new technological advance, the elimination of women becomes easier and more efficient.

In January 2006, Renuka Choudhary, the flamboyant Minister for Women and Child Welfare said at a press conference, 'Indian women are more endangered than tigers'. Given the pace at which things were moving, she could have easily added fifty years from now they might be deader than dodos.

6

The Law and the Lawless

'Yes, of course I know it is against the law,' Renu said. She had a faraway look in her eyes, as if she no longer cared what happened to her. She was holding her six-year-old daughter Pinky close to her. Maybe she thought I would snatch Pinky away.

We were sitting on a bench in one of the many parks that sprawl across the length and breadth of Chandigarh. It was a cold winter evening in 2005. One of those evenings when darkness falls fast. The joggers walked briskly up and down the well-laid cobbled tracks. Groups of senior citizens were sitting around on the benches taking in the air. Beside us a group of young children, mostly Sikh boys, were playing a boisterous game.

Renu had been reluctant to talk to me. I had to go through several layers of contacts to reach her. Finally, she agreed on condition of anonymity. Since her husband was a government servant, I could neither reveal her real name nor give any indication as to where she lived or who she was. Renu was one of the many women who had undergone the trauma of multiple illegal abortions over a period of five years.

Twenty-eight-year-old Renu lived in a comfortable middle class home in Chandigarh. Her husband had a good job and they owned a house and a car. Her mother-in-law who lived with them was a retired schoolteacher. Renu too had worked as a teacher for a while, but her multiple abortions in quest of a son had left her ill and exhausted. Now she just stayed home waiting to get pregnant so that she could try once more.

Over the last five years, Renu had had varied experiences. 'In the beginning it was not so tough,' she said. 'We knew the doctor at the scan centre. He indicated to us by signal that the baby was a girl. We went to the clinic that he suggested and had the foetus removed. It was simple. My health was also good at that time. The next two times were also okay, except that I got very tired and had to give up my job. My husband said having a son was more important than having a job. But when I had my last scan done three months ago there was some trouble. An NGO had complained against the scan centre and the police were watching all the patients. We had to produce false medical certificates.'

The worst was yet to come. She had to go in the middle of the night to a different clinic for the abortion. Since all the patients were being watched, the 'providers' of the abortion package did not want problems. Renu had no choice as she was already into it neck deep. They threatened her that her husband would get into trouble because he was a government servant. Afraid that he might lose his job, she went on a frightening midnight trip to an unknown clinic on the outskirts of Chandigarh.

'I am not getting any younger and my health is failing. I don't know how many more times I can do this,' Renu said. Four abortions in five years. I was shocked. And Renu was an educated woman living in a modern city. Was she so powerless? Was she so indifferent to the law?

'Law? What law?' she asked in a matter-of-fact manner. 'Will the law come to my help if I get thrown out of my house because I had one more daughter? Will the law help me if my husband marries again because he wants a son? Can the law stop society from looking down on me because I have no sons?'

'And you?' I asked. 'Do you want a son?'

'Yes,' she replied firmly. 'Unless I have a son, I cannot be happy. I want a son.'

'Even if it is against the law to have a sex-selective scan and abortion?'

She nodded again. 'Yes,' she repeated. 'I want a son.'

'More than 90 per cent of them are aware of the law,' Rainuka Dagar told me the next day as I sat with her in her neat little office room at the Institute for Development and Communication in Chandigarh. 'I don't think any woman who goes for a sex selection scan thinks it is legally allowed.' She pointed out to me that between 2002 and 2003 every ninth household in the state had acknowledged having had sex selective abortion done following ante-natal sex determination tests. Sex selective abortions had merely replaced female infanticide, which was historically the accepted method of disposing of unwanted girl children.

'In the old days they would sedate the newborn with a drop of opium and bury her alive in a mud pot,' she said. 'Now they scan the uterus and abort her before she is born. Pointing to female foeticide as the cause of the adverse sex ratio trivialises the issue. The adverse sex ratio in Punjab is a historical phenomenon. Prenatal diagnostic tests have added to the decline. They have not caused son preference.'

She pointed out that Punjab and Haryana had some of the most proactive programmes in the country. Yet the sex ratios in these two states were continuing to spiral downwards. The problem, therefore, was not with the law or its implementation. It was systemic. It could not be tackled by law alone because as long as the women themselves felt their lives were miserable until they had sons, they would not hesitate to break the law. For the lot of the woman to improve socially so many things had to change.

'First of all,' she said, 'the woman should not be viewed as the symbolic repository of tradition and culture. She has to be recognized as an equal. The power hierarchy has to change. Institutions like dowry and honour killing have to go. The whole phenomenon has to be tackled. Everything in one go. It can't be done piecemeal.'

In order to achieve this, a lot of resources had to be pumped in. Law enforcement was a part of the package, and though it was an important element, she felt the other problems had to be addressed alongside. Or else, the law would be ineffective. Rainuka Dagar's analysis was absolutely correct, but was it practical? Was there any government in existence, which actually had the capacity or the will to tackle 'everything at one go'?

I wished there was. It was like wishing for a magic wand. One swish and no more power hierarchies. Another and hey presto, no more disempowered women. Dreams. Dreams. One day later, I was back to ground reality. I was sitting in on a small embroidery class for women in Balongi village in Ropar district. This district had one of the worst sex ratios in Punjab. Manjit Singh of the Family Planning Association was talking to the women about scanning and female foeticide.

These were women who could not even imagine the concepts Rainuka Dagar and I had been talking about the previous day. For them living within the power hierarchy was a fact of life. They knew nothing about empowerment or identity. All they knew was that they did not want daughters. Daughters brought sorrow. Sons earned them a place in society. Manjit Singh and his colleagues had been talking to women like these for years now, trying to convince them to keep their daughters.

'The scan,' he said, 'has a good quality and an evil quality. It can be used to monitor the health of the child in your womb. That is its good quality. It can also be used to find out the sex of the child. That is its evil quality. Now, how many of you know that the evil scan is illegal? Put your hands up.'

All the hands went up. They all knew it was illegal. The women in this embroidery class came from lower-middle-class families. They were housewives with basic education who had come here in the hope of learning some income-generating activity. As they listened to Manjit Singh, they worked away at the embroidery pieces in their hands. They had the look of women who had heard it all many times before.

'Killing the girl child in your womb is equal to murder,' Manjit Singh said. 'You know that don't you?'

All the heads nodded.

'Then why do you do it?' he asked. 'Why do you allow it to happen? After all getting a sex selective scan done is a choice you voluntarily take. You have to make an effort to get it done. It is not like buying a vegetable off the cart of a street vendor who comes to your doorstep. You have to go in search of a doctor who will perform this illegal act. You have to want it. You have to decide to get the abortion done. And all the time you know it is against the law. So, why do you do it?'

The women remained silent. 'Is it because the control is always with the men?' Manjit Singh asked. 'Is it because you cannot decide for yourselves?'

'Because we cannot live in our *sasural* (in-laws' house) unless we produce sons,' said Kusum, a timid looking woman in her thirties. She was looking down at the cloth in her hand.

'After I had my daughter, I was under great pressure to produce a son. My husband's younger brother's wife had two sons before I had my first son. My life was miserable until I had my son.'

'If you don't have a son, you are nothing,' said an older woman sitting next to her. 'If you have two sons, it is like having two eyes. If you have one son you are half blind. If you have two daughters you are totally blind.'

'So will you have a sex selective scan and abortion even if it is illegal?' Manjit Singh asked. 'Do you not mind breaking the law?'

The women remained silent. It was worrying. Why did people have so much contempt for the law? What was this law which was being broken so easily by ordinary men and women, by doctors and midwives, by laboratories and hospitals across the length and breadth of the country? Why was it being flouted so blatantly?

Prior to the Pre-Natal Diagnostic Techniques (Regulation and Prevention of Misuse) Act (PNDT Act) enacted in 1994, determining the sex of the child or having a gender selective abortion was not illegal. The PNDT Act was the end result of a campaign which was started in 1986 by women's groups and health activists. In 1988, the Maharashtra government had formulated a similar Act at the state level. It took six more years for the Central Act to be passed. It was a pretty comprehensive piece of legislation for its time. According to the PNDT Act, pre-natal diagnostic techniques could be used only for detecting genetic abnormalities, congenital malformations or sex-linked disorders. The establishments that were allowed to conduct these tests, the professionals who could conduct them and the conditions under which they could be done were all clearly outlined under the Act. It also specified the pre-requisites to be fulfilled before the tests were conducted, the administrative structures required to monitor and implement its provisions and the procedure for registration of the establishments coming under its purview.

Using these techniques for pre-natal sex determination leading to female foeticide invited punishment in the form of imprisonment, fine and suspension of registration for medical practitioners. Those who sought such information as well as those who gave it could be punished. By 2000, though the Act had been in place for half a dozen years, things had gone from bad to worse.

There were any number of theories as to why this had happened. Many NGOs and activists put the blame squarely on the government. Enacting legislation was not enough, they said. Monitoring its implementation was even more important. This was where the state governments and health authorities had failed miserably.

Some new problems had also cropped up. By 2000, a number of new tests as well as New Reproductive Technologies (NRT), which could be used for sex selection had come in which were not under the purview of the 1994 PNDT Act. The providers of these new technologies were openly advertising their services in the popular media. Obviously there were a lot of new loopholes to be covered up.

In February 2000, Dr Sabu George in his capacity as an individual activist along with two NGOs, CEHAT and MASUM, filed a Public Interest Litigation (PIL) in the Supreme Court. The PIL sought to activate the Central and State governments to rigorously implement the central legislation. It also wanted pre-conception or during-conception sex-selection techniques and other new reproductive technologies to be brought under the purview of the PNDT Act. It pointed out that the government of

India had to be well informed and move with the times as, every day, new techniques were being evolved. The State governments were blamed for not monitoring the implementation of the Act that had led to a worsening of the situation. For example, in Tamil Nadu alone, the PIL said, more than 200 applications for registration of ultrasound clinics were waiting to be processed by the State Appropriate Authority named as per the PNDT Act. If they were not processed, the clinics would begin to operate without authorization. It also pointed out that the Appropriate Authorities in the various states had failed to prosecute the clinics that were 'with impunity advertising sex selection including Pre-Genetic Diagnosis (PGD)'.

In 2003, acting on the orders passed by the Supreme Court, the PNDT Act was amended. It was now known as the PCPNDT Act and it covered all kinds of pre-conception and prenatal diagnostic techniques. It brought under its purview some neglected areas like regulating the sale of equipment capable of detecting the sex of the foetus. It also specified under what circumstances diagnostic tests could be conducted on a pregnant woman and laid down certain strict rules regarding advertising of sex-selection techniques as well as services. Under the amended Act, it became mandatory to have a signboard in all ultrasound centres announcing that the detection and revealing of the sex of the foetus was illegal.

In 2005, demographer Ashish Bose was asked by journalist Madhu Gurung whether the amended PNDT Act had helped to check the spiralling adverse sex ratio.

'Without insulting the Supreme Court order,' he replied, 'it has not helped. How can anything help against demographic fundamentalism? How can anyone question why sons are required over girls?'

He told her he was not opposed to the law as it created

'an enabling environment to create awareness against female foeticide'. But he felt that basically it was not possible to implement the PNDT Act.

'The Supreme Court has ordered that all ultrasound machines have to be registered. But who will supervise this— the chief medical officer, who is also a doctor? How can he complain against other doctors?' he asked. 'Our doctors are cleverer than our policemen,' he pointed out. 'Our law demands evidence and not a single one has been caught with anything incriminating. Sex determination tests are the chief money-spinners.'

Asked what the ideal government policy should be, he said, 'One suggestion that I have given the government is to hire private detectives who should collect incriminating information against doctors who flout the PNDT Act, something like *Tehelka* . . . create a stir to get people working and rethinking'.

This was becoming more and more complex. The law could not be implemented unless attitudes changed and attitudes would not change unless the law was enforced. I felt I was stuck in some sort of a mystic maze with no way out. That was until I spoke to Dr Sabu George.

'You are wrong. How do you say it is an attitudinal problem? It is not an attitudinal problem,' Sabu George said over the phone. He sounded angry. 'These are all created attitudes. Let us be very clear. What we are seeing now is organized genocide.' It was the winter of 2005. I had contacted Sabu George because he was an active and vocal champion of a female's right to be born.

Sabu George had a lot of field experience as he had spent many years studying female child neglect in the villages of North Arcot in Tamil Nadu. His papers and articles on female infanticide and foeticide in Tamil Nadu, Punjab and Haryana were based on material he had gathered firsthand, while living in villages in these states. They gave a ground-level perspective of the situation across the country. In fact, when I contacted him for the first time, he was somewhere on the road in Haryana in between villages. I found that Sabu George was very clear about who was to blame and how the law should be enforced. According to him, son-preference resulting in female infanticide had existed in some pockets of India for a very long time. But it had remained confined to these pockets. It was only after the corrupt medical practitioners stepped into the arena with their sex detection technologies that the elimination of women became akin to mass genocide. Sex selection he pointed out was big business now. And in this business everything was acceptable. Including criminality.

'When criminality becomes the norm,' he said, 'Women are devalued.'

There was no point in blaming the women, he said, because they were mere pawns in the game. In this case, even education did not help them. Women from the privileged sections of society were, in fact, worse off. In prosperous South Delhi, for instance, he pointed out one in every six girls was eliminated. This, he said, showed that the privileged section was setting the worst standards. He was not for stopping medical technology. He only wanted to prevent its misuse. 'If we do not stop medical malpractice immediately,' he said, 'there won't be any women left. We have no time. It has to be done at once.'

He pointed a finger at major multinationals who were making and marketing these machines. They were actually marketing genocide by not keeping a proper check over the machines they sold. Their aggressive marketing strategies, he said, had resulted in their selling machines in a haphazard and uncontrolled manner to unqualified and unscrupulous persons.

'It is ironic and shocking,' he said, 'That a multinational company which sells these machines without any thought also has a foundation for the girl child.'

His solution? Do not legitimize these crimes of violence. Prosecute the people who misuse the technology, no matter what their standing in society is. Target the corrupt doctors, technicians and agents who knowingly use and sell the technology for sex selection, rather than the misdirected people who go to them for using their service. He felt even CEOs of the multinationals should be prosecuted for negligence.

This was surely not as easy as it sounded. When and how did the ultrasound machine, which was a diagnostic tool, turn into a murder weapon? Obviously, when the multinationals made the machines they had not intended this. When then did the process get corrupted? Did the manufacturers blindly push the machines into the market because they had sky-high sales targets?

'It is a kind of double-edged problem,' said Dr M.D. Ravi, a paediatrician from Mysore with twenty-five years of experience. 'For me now, the ultrasound has become almost as indispensable as a stethoscope. As a number of my patients come from middle and low income groups, the cost is important. That means for a person like me, cheap ultrasound is an absolute necessity. This cost benefit can occur only if more machines are made and sold. But unless the sale of the machines is monitored, I can see that there is definitely a potential problem.'

Ravi used a medical analogy to explain why the problem of tackling corruption in this case was so complex. 'When a disease vector is capable of surviving only in human beings,' he said, 'it is possible to control it. It can be controlled and even eradicated by vaccinating human beings. But, when the vector is capable of surviving in other life forms like animals or birds, the problem goes out of control. Like for example bird flu. When there are multiple points of attack, eradication becomes so difficult it almost seems impossible. In the case of female foeticide, the disease vector has spread across varied segments, which is why control and eradication are problems.'

Changing social structures was a long term process, he said. So the only immediate interim solution would be to strictly regulate the use of the machines. He felt that this was the most practical point of intervention. Meanwhile, social scientists were beginning to point out some new problems which had arisen because of the legislation which had pushed the entire 'business' underground.

In January 2006, I was in Ahmedabad. A kite festival was going on. Shops overflowed with kites of various sizes, shapes and hues. Up in the sky, birds and kites competed for space. The atmosphere was warm and festive. So much freedom. So much joy. How could people not want girls here?

Gujarat has one of the worst sex ratios in the country. The urban CSR was just 827 and in Mahasena district close to Ahmedabad, it was an abysmal 798. And even that figure, according to my sources was high. No one knew any longer how many female foetuses were actually being aborted.

Inside the spacious book-lined office of Leela Visaria, Director of the Gujarat Institute of Development Research in Ahmedabad, I felt the cold creeping into my bones again as we discussed the chilling situation that seemed to be growing worse by the day. Like Sabu George, Leela Visaria too had a lot of field experience. She had lived and worked among the Jadeja Rajputs of Kutch who practiced female infanticide. She had investigated female infanticide in Tamil Nadu, Gujarat and Punjab and written several papers on foeticide and other forms of discrimination against the girl child.

Now she was worried about the new problems that had cropped up after sex-selective abortion became illegal. The sex determination test had not disappeared, Leela Visaria pointed out. It had merely gone underground. As a fallout, access to safe legitimate abortions had become jeopardized. 'After the PNDT Act came into effect, we can no longer get exact information on how many sex detection tests are performed and who performs them and how many female foetuses are aborted,' she said.

In India abortion has been legal since 1972. A woman can get a legal abortion done if her pregnancy carries the risk of grave physical injury or endangers her mental health in any way. It is allowed, for example, if the pregnancy is due to a contraceptive failure or is a result of rape. The foetus can also be aborted if it is found to be physically or mentally abnormal. Recording an abortion or MTP (Medical Termination of Pregnancy), as it is rather euphemistically called has always been mandatory. With the new law in place it became essential to record all the details. The result was confusion. Most of the women who wanted an MTP were not even sure whether they were legally entitled to have one or not. Corrupt medical practitioners cashed in on this.

'The problem,' Leela Visaria said, 'is that couples no longer understand what is legal and what is illegal. It has all got mixed up.' She felt that the confusion arose because there was such a thin line dividing the legal from the illegal. Abortion was a woman's legal right but the elimination of a foetus on the basis of its sex was illegal as it violated a girl's right to be born. How many couples understood or accepted this difference? A woman could also legally abort her foetus if it was found to be 'abnormal'. But what was normal and what was abnormal? Women, who wanted to abort a female foetus, often used the same justifications as women who wanted to get rid of an 'abnormal' one. According to Leela Visaria, in the minds of the parents, a medically abnormal foetus and a female foetus were accorded 'similar status'. Both of them were 'sociologically' undesirable.

To such parents, she said, 'like a medically abnormal foetus, a female foetus is also expensive to maintain if allowed to be born. It is less productive than normal persons, can be detrimental to the parents' emotional and financial well-being, and is on many accounts better not being born.' So, she said, they begin to feel that if a medically unviable foetus could be legally aborted why not a genetically unviable one?

Legal or illegal, who cared? To the parents, eliminating the girl child was a social necessity. To the doctors and clinics it was good business. A VHAI (Voluntary Health Association of India) study surveyed the providers of services like ultrasound tests and abortions. It found that almost all those who were surveyed knew that pre-natal sex selection tests were illegal. They had even displayed the mandatory boards saying the tests were illegal. Yet many of them revealed the sex of the child to their clients either because the clients 'pressurized' them to do so or because they would lose business otherwise. Some of the providers argued that even if they did not reveal the sex, the client would go to another clinic and find out.

In May 2005, *Times of India* correspondent Gur Kirpal Singh came out with a distressing piece of news. 'Many doctors in Punjab,' he wrote 'keen to make a quick buck are aborting male foetuses when parents approach them for ante-natal sex determination.' Apparently the doctors offered a 'package deal' costing between Rs 8000 and Rs 15,000. Before the implementation of the PNDT Act, the test cost just Rs 500. The cost went up after the test and abortion became illegal. A nurse told Singh, 'In many cases, even if the foetus is male, the parents are told it is female so that the clinic can earn the abortion fee.'

The health secretary told him that because of the PNDT Act, the doctors got rid of the incriminating foetus and without it no one could prove whether the aborted child was male or female. The parents could not speak out even if they suspected foul play, because under the Act, even they could be punished.

Vijaya Pushkarna, Chandigarh correspondent of *The Week* magazine spoke of one more unfortunate fallout.

'Female infanticide is making a comeback in Punjab and Haryana,' she said. 'As it becomes more and more difficult for women to have a sex selective scan and abortion, they are falling back on the old methods.' Pushkarna spoke of the bodies of unwanted girl babies surfacing periodically on the roadside in rural Haryana or in rivers and streams of fertile Punjab. She told me about a sweeper in a doctor's house in Bhatinda who was caught throwing two foetuses into a dustbin. She said more people were now either killing or abandoning their girl children.

Meanwhile, in Chandigarh, Dr Dahiya, of Punjab's State Appropriate Authority, was going after violators of the PNDT Act with the fervor of a crusader. It had all started when he was working as a civil surgeon in Faridabad. When Dr Dahiya got evidence against a doctor who had violated the PNDT Act, he registered a case against him. This became the first ever case to be registered in India against a person for violating this particular Act. The Faridabad doctor had powerful political connections and Dr Dahiya was pressurized to withdraw the case and apologize. He refused. As a 'reward', he was transferred. Later on he became a member of the State Appropriate Authority and spearheaded an aggressive campaign against corrupt medical practitioners.

In an interview to *The Week*, Dr Dahiya said, 'By the time we convince and sensitize society, very few girls will be left in the country. So strict implementation on the PNDT Act alone will help arrest the trend.' As a representative of the State Appropriate Authority, Dr Dahiya had his own flamboyant way of working. He conducted sting operations with high profile media coverage. He got doctors to admit their guilt on tape. His exploits were splashed all over the newspapers and magazines. TV channel crews followed him on his raids.

His strategy worked. Soon he had nearly twenty-five cases booked under the PNDT Act. He got 786 ultrasound centres and sixty-six Genetic Counselling Centres registered in the state. Subsequent to the raids, forty-three ultrasound machines were sealed and more than forty registrations were suspended under the PNDT Act for various violations.

In March 2006 a sub-divisional judicial magistrate in Haryana sentenced the proprietor of Dr Anil's ultrasound clinic in Faridabad. Dr Anil Sabhani and his assistant Kartar Singh to two years imprisonment and a fine of Rs 5,000 each for violating the PNDT Act. This became the first ever conviction in India under this Act. The case had taken five years to reach this stage.

In 2001 a team of government doctors had sent three decoy patients to Dr Sabhani. The investigating team managed to get solid proof against the doctors. They had a video recording of the doctor revealing the sex of their unborn babies to the decoy patients. They also recovered incriminating marked notes from the pockets of the two doctors. The fact remained that though the PNDT Act had been in place for twelve years, this was the very first conviction. The problem was there were no complainants. It was like walking into a spider's web. Since the 'customers' were as guilty as the 'providers' anyone who wandered into the nexus got stuck.

In February 2006, in an article in *Outlook*, Chander Suta Dogra wrote about the interwoven nexus which was continuing to play havoc with the sex ratios in Punjab.

'Everywhere in Nawanshahr district,' he wrote, 'people talk about a well-entrenched network of educated "dais", nurses, midwives and doctors, encompassing private practitioners and those from the government's health department, who facilitate violations of the Act with impunity.'

He quoted Paramjit Kaur, the child development project officer of Banga block, who admitted that health department officials, particularly the Auxiliary Nurse Midwives (ANMs), Lady Health Visitors (LHVs), supervisors and doctors were deeply involved in the business because 'these are the people who are intimately connected with pregnant women as part of their duties.'

Some sordid details of the nexus came to light when Krishan Kumar, a dynamic deputy commissioner was posted in Nawanshahr district. When he conducted detailed surveys of villages which came under his purview, he found to his shock that some of them had a sex ratio of less than 450 girls to 1000 boys. This was much lower than the figures projected in the 2001 census. He decided to take an aggressive stance.

At a meeting of private and government doctors, which he convened to discuss the situation, accusations and counter-accusations flew high. And lots of new questions came up. The Chief Medical Officer of the government hospital and his radiologist wife were accused of scanning pregnant women for sex selection by a woman gynaecologist in private practice, who was also vice-president of the local chapter of the Indian Medical Association (IMA). She said that the husband and wife, both government doctors, conducted sex determination scans and then referred their customers to specific *dais*, ANMs and doctors for a commission. However, the accuser herself had been accused of violating the PNDT Act and her clinic had been sealed. She claimed she was victimized because she refused to perform an abortion on a woman sent by the doctor couple. They asked her to produce evidence.

In another case in Naura village in Naushahr district, Manjit Kaur and her husband Santokh Singh were accused of aborting their female foetus at a nursing home in a neighbouring district. Since Nawanshahr had become 'too hot' to conduct an abortion Manjit went to a relative's place in nearby Hoshiarpur district and got her pregnancy terminated at Shashi Nursing Home and Scan Centre. Investigations revealed some interesting information about the doctor couple who owned this nursing home. The wife was a former government doctor and her husband was the district Family Planning Officer. More importantly, he also headed the district committee constituted to 'enforce' the PNDT Act.

In the districts of Punjab, the law, it seemed, was made only to be broken. Pregnant women from villages located close to towns just got into a bus and got the scan and abortion done in relative anonymity. It cost a little more, but if they chose their medical centres carefully, they were safe. Women living in remote villages depended on nurses and *dais* who worked as middlewomen for the scan centres and nursing homes. Since these were local women, they had the full confidence of the villagers. They would either escort the pregnant women to the closest 'safe' scan centre or contact doctors with mobile scans to come to the village. They would pocket the commission and often perform the abortion themselves. Obviously it was good business. There was a very definite link between the presence of a nurse or trained dai in a village and its low sex ratio. So, like the 'good' scan which had turned 'evil', the agents of birth had become the agents of death. The very law which had been enacted for the good of women had, in the hands of the lawless, become a blackmail weapon to be used against them.

7

Who Wants Daughters?

The Mahavir Mandir in Sunderpur in Gujarat was a small colourful little temple. On a sunny Sunday afternoon in January 2006, the local Nehru Yuvak Kendra (NYK) had arranged a meeting on female foeticide for all the women in the village.

Sunderpur looked like a prosperous village; green and tranquil. We drove to the temple via a kutcha country road watched by huge, healthy buffaloes placidly chewing cud. Here, people were well off and educated. It looked like the last place on earth where one would expect to find a group of women who would openly and defiantly say they just did not want girls.

Earlier, we had had lunch with Nirmal, the smart young NYK coordinator. His four sisters and mother had cooked a grand meal. They all looked confident and happy.

'I don't know why the villagers don't want girls,' Nirmal's father said. 'We are so proud of our daughters.' His neighbours obviously did not feel the same way because this village had a child sex ratio well below 800.

Sunderpur was a village close to Gandhinagar in Gujarat. It lay in the heart of a large tract covering Ahmedabad, Mehsana, Gandhinagar, Visnagar, Mansa and Unjha where the CSRs were well below 800. The amazing thing was that the villages here were not part of some impoverished rural hinterland. This was a well-connected, prosperous fertile part of Gujarat, inhabited by wealthy farmers. Literacy levels were high. The young volunteers who had organized the meeting and lived in the village had all been to college. They carried cell phones and talked about internet connectivity and cell phone towers in interior villages.

The Patels, who were the dominant community here, had a history of migration. They had relatives scattered all over the world. Many of their relatives owned motels in the US. Others worked as software engineers in big cities or ran flourishing business empires. The ones who stayed back continued to tend the land, which was initially responsible for their prosperity.

Since it was a Sunday, the turnout was good. Children ran around playing hide and seek among the granite pillars in the temple courtyard where the meeting was convened. The volunteers of the NYK had put up their banner and distributed packets of savoury mixture to the women who sat on colourful cotton mats. The mood was definitely festive.

The small team from the Ahmedabad NGO Chetna, which had arranged my visit, was trying to get the women to sit down and maintain a semblance of silence. Since I didn't know Gujarati, Bhumika, the young researcher from Chetna had volunteered to be my translator. The village women knew her well and exchanged pleasantries with her. Bhumika got things going by speaking about the evil of female foeticide and the repercussions it could have on the community. The young men in these areas had a severe problem. The sex ratios had dipped so low, they could no longer find girls to marry.

The previous day we had been to Moucha village in Prantij block, about 100 kilometers away from Ahmedabad. In the 324 families belonging to the Darbar community who lived in the village, there were 123 men of marriageable age who could not find brides. A little further on, in Upkal village, the wife of the deputy sarpanch who was a Patel, had begged us to find a bride for her son. Women of marriageable age had obviously become scarce in every community in these parts. The fact that young men in these areas could not find brides within their own communities was a major issue now.

Bhumika knew the right buttons to press. It was a good speech. Obviously she had spoken about this many times before, and obviously the women had heard it many times too.

They listened politely at first. And then, the murmuring began. The women were becoming increasingly bored and restless. They began chatting with each other. The decibel level became louder by the minute. The chatter rose to a din. Bhumika's gentle voice got drowned. 'Listen,' she cried, clapping her hands and trying to get their attention back to what she was saying. But the women of Sunderpur were in no mood to listen to something they were not convinced about. The sound level rose to a crescendo. Even the pigeons which were peacefully pecking at grains in the temple courtyard fluttered their wings and rose up in protest.

'Listen,' Bhumika shouted now, trying to make herself heard above the cacophony. 'Listen, our guest has some questions for all of you.' A couple of older women sitting on the mats in the front row stood up and shouted too. 'Quiet. Let her speak. Let our guest also speak.' Slowly the chatter died down. There was a semblance of silence. Bhumika translated my questions into Gujarati.

'How many of you know that scanning to find out the sex of your child is against the law?' she asked. All the hands in the audience went up very promptly. 'How many of you know that the scan is also used for medical purposes?' she asked. The women looked at each other and smiled. All the hands went up again.

'How many of you have had a scan when you were pregnant?' Bhumika asked. The women started laughing and chattering. Not a single hand went up. The chatter rose by several decibels.

'Listen, listen,' Bhumika said, clapping her hands. 'Listen to me. You have to have a scan to find out if the baby is doing well. That is not against the law. But it is illegal to find out the sex of your baby and then abort it.'

The women laughed. Of course they knew that.

'So do you mean to say you have never had a scan done?' Bhumika asked.

'Where did we have scan in our time?' a beautiful old lady asked smiling. 'All this scan business is new.'

'But what about your daughters? Your daughters-in-law?'

'As if they listen to us,' another old lady said. 'They go to the doctor with their husbands and they decide if they want to have daughters or not.'

'But, don't you advise them?'

'No, no,' another woman said. 'Why should we? We ourselves don't want daughters. Why should we produce more daughters to suffer like us?'

I felt weary. How many times had I heard this sentence and in how many different languages? Did they really believe this to be true? I remembered that nameless old woman in Alligundam who had said, 'Better to kill her before she knows this miserable life. Better to send her straight to heaven rather than make her endure this beating and kicking around. What joy have we got by staying alive?'

But the women of Sunderpur looked different. They were not caught in that vicious cycle of poverty, debt and death. How could they say the same thing?

'But all of you look so happy,' I said. 'Why do you think your daughters will suffer? They may also be happy like you.'

'They will suffer in their *sasural*,' one woman said.

'Our society is so bad. They can get attacked even on the way to school,' said another. 'I don't want to bring up a daughter in this dangerous society.'

'Whose daughter has been attacked on the way to school?'

'No one. Not in our village. But, we read the papers. It happens all the time,' some of the women said.

'How many of you are suffering in your *sasural*?'

Not a single hand went up.

'They are afraid to say because their mothers-in-law are sitting next to them,' one young woman giggled, clutching her two young sons close to her.

'Oh, she is alright. She has two sons. She will not suffer in her *sasural*,' another young woman said. 'If she had two daughters the story would be different.'

'Do women have problems with their in-laws if they have only daughters?'

'We ourselves don't want daughters,' a woman shouted from the back.

'Do you have problems between mothers-in-law and daughters-in-law in your houses?'

'We are like sisters,' some women said.

'They are like our daughters,' others said.

'Then why do you think your daughters will suffer?'

'There is a chance that they might suffer,' one woman shouted. 'We don't want to take that chance. Others may not be like us. They might torture our daughters.'

'We don't want daughters,' a woman in the first row repeated very firmly.

'No, no, no.' All the hands shook in unison.

'No, no. We don't want daughters.'

All the women were shouting, shaking their hands in the air. The little girls and boys stopped playing among the pillars. They started laughing, thinking it was all a game. 'No, no,' the children shouted imitating their mothers. They didn't even know what they were saying no to. We were stunned. They were almost treating it like a joke, but we could see they were very serious. They were very sure. They did not want daughters.

'So, what will you do?' Bhumika asked, exasperated. 'Will you abort your daughters?'

'Yes, yes,' they shouted.

Bhumika was despondent as we drove out of the village. 'Our message does not seem to have reached,' she said. 'I never expected this reaction from them.'

The Patels of Gujarat were actually migrants from Haryana and adjoining areas, which now belonged to Pakistan. They came around 200 years ago to settle down in this fertile part of the country and cultivate the land. Even their look and stature was different from the native Gujaratis. The parts of the country they came from, female infanticide was traditionally practised.

Sociologists pointed out that almost all the communities which had a tradition of female infanticide had now taken to scientific means of elimination in a big way. For example, the Kallars of Usilampatti deep down in south India, were originally a nomadic group from north India where female infanticide was probably a tradition. Similarly, the Jadejas of Kutch, who also practiced female infanticide, came originally from Rajasthan where it was again a tradition. Originally adversity made these communities get rid of their daughters after they were born. Now prosperity had helped them to find more efficient means to continue the practice of eliminating their daughters, even before they were born.

In Punjab and Haryana, the area from which the Patels

originally came, girl babies were 'traditionally' and ceremoniously fed opium and buried alive in a sealed earthen pot. In Gujarat, the 'tradition' among the Patels was called 'doodh pithi'. Here the opium and the pot remained the same. The method of elimination was slightly different. After the just-born infant girl was given a drop of opium, she was ceremonially drowned in an earthen pot of milk. Girls had always been scarce in this community, but now with the growing popularity and availability of the scan, they were in danger of becoming extinct.

On 1 January 2006, just two weeks before I visited the villages, the leaders of the Patel community had organized an unusual programme called the 'Maha Laddu Prasad Karikram' in Surat. Nearly 50,000 kilograms of sweet boondi was prepared and made into laddus. This 'prasad' was packed into 35 lakh boxes and sent to every single Patel family in the state, with a note asking them to take a vow that they would never again kill a female child. At the Surat function, 12 lakh Patels had gathered. All of them went on stage and vowed to end female foeticide in their community. Leaders from various other communities who were there also took the pledge. In every village we visited, people were talking about the 'laddu prasad' which they had received. But, was it going to make a difference?

In Anandpur village, almost all the families had received boxes of laddus. The meeting this time was at night in a small village hall. Before we entered the hall, a group of influential men from the village sat around on chairs, talking to me about the alarming sex ratios which continued to fall.

'We don't know how this happened,' said Kalabhai Dwarakdas Patel, husband of the village sarpanch. 'Ours is one of the most prosperous districts. We have a high literacy rate. We were one of the first districts to accept family planning. We all love our daughters. We treat them just like we treat our sons. No difference. We educate them. Sons don't study. They don't look after their parents in their old age.'

Then what had happened? Why was the sex ratio low?

At the meeting, we asked people whether getting the boxes of laddu made any difference to them. Did they now feel more obliged to keep their daughters? The Patel women of Anandpur were a more subdued lot. They just shook their heads silently. They looked puzzled. 'Why should it make a difference? We never had anything against girls,' one woman said. 'Girls are more loving than boys.'

I did my usual test. I asked all the women with only two sons to raise their hands. There were over a dozen. However, there were no women at all with just two daughters. There were some with a son and a daughter or two sons and a daughter. As we walked out into the moonlit night, breathing in the fresh village air, some of the women came and spoke to me. 'We don't have anything against daughters,' one of them said. 'Daughters are gentle. They study better. They even care for their parents more than sons do. But we are not rich people. We cannot afford more than one daughter.'

As more of them collected around us and talked in an informal manner, we realized that the very fact that they were all reasonably well educated and informed had made them take certain decisions which had had a definite impact on the sex ratio. Almost all the women felt that raising a daughter was fraught with difficulties. She had to be protected from assault. Even though they wanted to educate their daughters, they were afraid to send them out alone in the evenings either to tuition class or to faraway colleges. Raising a daughter was also expensive. Even though they claimed they had no dowry system, they ended up paying a lot of money towards wedding expenses as well as for buying gold and household goods. Often families with daughters had to sell a portion of land to meet these expenses.

Therefore, almost all the women said that after one daughter they definitely liked to choose the sex of the next child. Since all of them were in favour of planned families, they said that they would like to balance the sex of the two children they had. However 'balancing' had its own meaning in these parts. If the first born was a son, they did not bother about the sex of the second one. If the first born was a daughter, they definitely went in for sex selection. So, a second son was always allowed to be born, but never a second daughter.

How did they get the illegal sex selective abortion done? Things were not like before, the women said. When the scan first made its appearance, doctors readily revealed the sex of the foetus to them. Now they had to go to 'friendly' doctors. Or to doctors who were relatives. These doctors verbally revealed the sex of the child. Getting an abortion done after that was not such a problem. There were any number of competent midwives and friendly neighbourhood clinics who could perform this operation.

'TV is partly to blame for this situation,' Dhani Behn said. 'Even in deep rural areas people have a TV and watch all the soap operas. Since the literacy level is low in villages, previously men and women did not know about all this scan-wan. Now they know more, so they do more to get rid of their girl children. Now all of them know about sex selective abortions and they are willing to travel from their villages to the nearest town to get it done.'

Dhani Behn was a bright Dalit woman who was a former sarpanch of Moucha village. She sat on a plastic chair sipping tea from her saucer in typical rural style during an informal discussion in the courtyard of the spacious hut belonging to the present sarpanch Passi Behn.

'Many of the soap operas give wrong messages,' Dhani Behn said. 'They continuously project women as weak creatures who are burdens to the family and make it appear as if all mothers-in-law have problems with their daughters-in-law. Naturally women feel they want to get rid of their daughters.'

Passi Behn sat quietly. She was certainly not dynamic like Dhani Behn. Nor did she have a specific opinion on any of the subjects we were discussing. She held her post because she was a woman. She let her menfolk do the talking. Her husband told us there was no discrimination against women in the village and that no one ever went for a sex determination scan. Passi Behn nodded her head in agreement.

'The sarpanch has four grown-up sons, so she had no problems,' one of the village women squatting on the mud floor remarked. 'Where will a person like me go? I am a daily wage earner. If I have more than one daughter I will drown in debt.'

Women had four sons, but in these days no one ever had four daughters. Why? We asked Passi Behn. She didn't reply. But her brother-in-law Prabhat Singh did.

'We are poor people,' he said. 'We live by cultivating the land. No one in this village has a government job. How can we afford to have more daughters?'

Jayanti Bhai Patel, the headmaster of the village high school, brought out the school register. There were 170 boys and 161 girls studying in his school. What was worrying was that even in this remote village, in every single age group there were less number of girls than boys. And, already there were a number of bachelors who could not find brides.

In Ahmedabad, Ila Pathak, member of the State Appropriate Authority pointed to a newspaper report of the 'laddu' programme in a local daily. Beside the report was a half-page 'letter from an unborn baby girl to her mother'. The baby begged the mother to let her be born. Such strategies only angered Ila Pathak. What was the use of appealing to the women to stop killing their unborn girl babies she asked, when they had absolutely no power over their own bodies. Ila Pathak had been in the arena of action for over twenty years. She had a fund of stories on her experiences in the field.

'In Ahmedabad there was a huge rally where 7000 women took an oath saying they would never kill their girl babies,' she said. 'I found it pointless. Most of the times, a woman does not even have the power to refuse to have sex when a husband demands it. From where do you think she will get the power to resist if he insists on a sex determination test? What will she do if he beats her or threatens to throw her out of the house if she bears a daughter?'

What about educated women? Employed women? Women who held positions of power? Were they not empowered enough to say we want to keep our daughters?

'It can be a very disturbing experience,' a senior woman minister in the Karnataka cabinet told me. 'Suddenly you realize you are in a very vulnerable position.'

It was February 2006 and we were travelling together in her car in Bangalore. We were returning from a meeting on projects to arrest female foeticide. We were talking about why even educated women get their female foetuses aborted.

'It is not enough if you are educated,' she said in a sad and reflective tone. 'What about the people who actually control your life? People like your husband and mother-in-law. What if they feel strongly that you must have a son? I know how it feels when you think that you can get thrown out of the house for bearing another daughter. Or that your husband can marry again to get a son to carry forward his lineage. It can be very frightening.'

Nearly twenty-five years ago, when she was already an MLA, this woman politician was expecting her second child. When her first child turned out to be a daughter, her mother-in-law was very upset. 'My husband is an only son and she was very particular that my next child should be a son,' she said. 'So, when I found out I was carrying twins, I became very tense. What if they both turned out to be daughters?'

So tense, in fact, that she wrote a letter to her husband saying that she knew his mother would throw her out of the house or get him married again if she had more daughters. But, she wrote, she had reconciled herself to this and would bring up all her daughters on her own. Since she had an MA degree, she had decided she would quit politics and take up a teacher's job if it was necessary. Her husband, she told me, had preserved that letter carefully. Reading it over and over again helped her even now to empathize with the women who went through this trauma. As it turned out, she had twin sons. But she always wonders what would have happened to her if they had been twin daughters.

My experience with the Patel women of Gujarat had only reinforced the growing feeling that education per se did not empower women. They might be educated and well-off, but they still viewed themselves as weak and vulnerable. Full-time homemakers in particular seemed to feel threatened by the outside world.

'How can we bring up daughters today? Society has become unsafe,' was a sentiment I heard often in Punjab, Haryana, Gujarat and Rajasthan.

In Punjab and Haryana this sentiment was particularly strong. These were vulnerable parts of the country where historically, the people had always been fighting off invaders.

The Jats of Punjab like the Rajputs of Rajasthan were a martial race. Men went to war leaving behind women who often became victims of the marauding conquerors. Female infanticide had its root in those bloody and unsafe times.

In 1947, the partition of India and Pakistan brought in its wake a wave of violence and bloodshed. Many women were brutally assaulted, forcibly plucked from their families and even killed. These events left traumatic scars on the collective memory of at least two generations. The families who were supposed to protect the honour of their women found they could do nothing in the face of such unbridled terror. And this deeply affected the psyche of the community as a whole.

After Independence, things settled down and there was a period of comparative peace and prosperity. However, even before the traumatized families could quite recover, terror reared its ugly head once more. In the 1980s and early 1990s, Punjab was in the grip of militants. And, as usual, the women were the worst hit.

Women and girls were easy prey for the militants. According to women who lived through those frightening times, sexual assault was a standard form of punishment even for minor crimes like violating dress or conduct codes. Like the marauding conquerors of yore, militants on the prowl would take women as hostages. Many women died in their custody. Even when they were released, they had to die a thousand more deaths as they were rejected by the society from which they came. Militancy took a definite toll. Girls even stopped going to school for fear they would be kidnapped.

Fatehgarh Sahib in Punjab has one of the lowest sex ratios in the state. Ironically, it is a district dominated by important shrines. The most important gurudwara is dedicated to a martyr: Fateh Singh, the youngest son of the tenth Sikh guru, Guru Gobind Singh.

The district, which is predominantly rural, has seen its sex ratios dropping steadily over the years. The adult sex ratio dropped from 871 in 1991 to 854 in 2001. The child sex ratio did much worse. From 874 in 1991, it dropped to 776 in 2001. Like many other places in Punjab, Fategarh Sahib had its share of terrorist activities. But why were the sex ratios dropping even further after peace returned to this part of the country? Peace and stability, I had thought would see a resurgence of women. Why did families still want to get rid of their unborn daughters?

I found out why when I spoke to a still-grieving mother in Fatehgarh Sahib. As we sat in her comfortable little home overlooking the fields, the woman, who wished to remain anonymous, spoke of the trauma she had been through when her only daughter was abducted, raped and killed by militants. She now lived with her sons and grandsons. But there were no daughters or granddaughters in her family.

'Yes. I have only sons and grandsons,' she said defiantly. 'I never again want a daughter in this family. The world is evil. Women cannot live here. We need sons to look after the land and keep the lineage alive. We do not need daughters. A daughter is like a flower. She can be crushed and ruined. Why should we produce daughters only to see them destroyed by this evil society?'

She had no faith in peace or in the ability of authorities to maintain peace. She had seen too much bloodshed in her family over the past three generations and the women, she concluded, were the worst hit. Daughters, she said, were burdens. It was better if they were never born.

I heard this sentiment echoed over and over again across the length and breadth of the country. Women and men who lived peaceful and prosperous lives still spoke of the 'burden' of bringing up vulnerable daughters in a society which could turn violent at any time. The 'educated' were also the most 'aware'. They were the ones who felt they were obliged to produce only sons.

The more I probed, the more I realized that generations of educated women from middle and high-income groups had been brainwashed into believing that they were duty bound to produce more sons. Since men as well as women thought that daughters were financial and emotional burdens, preventing them from being born was the only way they could ensure the peace and prosperity of the family.

A son would bring in wealth. A daughter would take it away. Too many children would erode the family's prosperity. So they had to strategize. They had to make sure they had the optimum number of children of the desired sex. Their own education and comfortable financial status helped them to strategize better. They used scientific advancement to their benefit and made sure no unwanted daughters were born.

Just as I was trying to come to terms with my bizarre finding, I came across a Delhi based study which gave muscle to this theory. A team of three researchers from the Christian Medical Association of India analysed sex ratios at birth (SRB) in hospitalized deliveries in Delhi. The result of this study, published in 2005, gave some interesting statistics about parents who went in for sex-selective abortions. Joe Varghese, Vijay Aruldas and Panniyammakal Jeemon studied the sex ratio at birth in eight large hospitals in Delhi for a ten-year period from 1993 to 2002. They looked at the socio-economic as well as the demographic background of the parents. And this is what they found.

The Sex Ratio at Birth (SRB) was the worst when both parents had a high school level of education. In that category the SRB was an abysmal 690. Whereas, when both parents had less than seven years of education, the SRB was a healthy 934. So, relatively uneducated parents did not choose the sex of their children. Was it because they did not know how? Or because they could not afford sex-selective abortions? Or because they genuinely did not discriminate against girl children?

Even when the educational status of the mother and father were analysed separately, the researchers found that higher educational levels had an adverse impact on the SRB. When the mother had less than ten years of education the SRB was 763. When she had more than a high school education it dropped to 741. When the father had a minimal education, the SRB was 840. If he had completed ten years of schooling, it came down to a very low 690. When both parents were graduates, there was a marginal improvement and the SRB was 813.

Then there was one more surprise. As the education levels of the parents went further up, the SRB amazingly decreased. For parents with a post-graduate qualification, it dropped to a shocking 769. Such highly educated parents in fact seemed to prefer to have just one single male child.

The researchers then took a look at the employment status of the parents and came up with more surprises. They found that the SRB for educated, employed mothers was 827 girls for 1000 boys. But, when educated mothers stayed at home, the SRB dropped to 787. This confirmed my own informal findings.

The researchers also found that if the mother was employed in a high-end job (i.e. a job which required years of professional training), she was more likely to keep her female child. Among the employed mothers, the SRB was lowest for women with low-paid jobs. So obviously the stay-at-home mothers and women in low-paid jobs were the ones who felt most obliged to eliminate their daughters. Was it because they were the ones who felt most disempowered themselves? And what about the fathers? Did their job status affect the SRB? Not much, the researchers found.

The SRB for fathers with high-end jobs was just 777, whereas fathers who were in business had an SRB of 796. Not much of a margin, but it did indicate that the job status of the father had not much of an impact on his preference for sons. In fact, when both the parents' employment status was taken into account, the worst ratio was found amongst parents where the father had a high-end job and the mother stayed at home. In this category, the SRB was just 743. On the other hand, if the mother was also employed, then this figure rose to 859. So, the poor and uneducated men and women were not really the ones who went in for sex selection. To the uninitiated, this was a real surprise.

The researchers concluded, 'Contrary to the popular perception, the educational status of the parents does not produce any desired result on the family's decisions to go in for sex-selective abortions.'

In Chandigarh, Rainuka Dagar told me that in Punjab and Haryana, the sex ratios were best among the scheduled castes and Dalits simply because they had no land and so they had no issues of family status, division of property and so on. To them, children, irrespective of their sex, meant more hands to bring in food and money.

Surveys conducted in 2001 in Punjab found that among the upper income group, 53 per cent of the families surveyed had gone in for pre-natal diagnostic tests. The percentage of families who admitted to using these tests went down in proportion to the decreasing income (and presumably education) levels. Among the low income group, just 19 per cent said they used the test.

On a warm winter's morning in 2005, I walked into a small anganwadi in Barhmajra, just outside Mohali in Punjab. I had visited quite a few such day care centres over the past week and the story had always been the same. In every anganwadi, in every school and on every playground, there were always more boys than girls. It had become so routine. In every village, in every locality, the men and women expressed the same ignorance. They never went in for sex selection they said. They didn't know why there were more boys than girls.

Maybe appearances were deceptive. Maybe the girls were not sent out to school or even out to play.

So, at Barhmajra, I really didn't expect anything different. I was almost about to leave after just a cursory glance. Since the children here belonged to immigrant labourers from Bihar and Orissa, the Sikh topknot was missing. At first glance I could not even make out how many boys and how many girls there were.

However, I was in for a pleasant surprise. The teacher in charge asked me to sit for a moment and brought out the register. I looked again, almost not believing what I saw. Out of the forty-five students in this little daycare centre, twenty-three were girls and only twelve were boys. Even more surprising in this day and age, seven of the girls were sisters. Seven girls in one family? This seemed to be a total anachronism in today's world. And that too in Punjab. In almost all the village anganwadis I had seen so far, the Sikh boys were prominent. The number of girls was markedly smaller. So, what made Barhmajra different?

Barhmajra was a largish rural slum of immigrants from Bihar and Orissa. The menfolk here travelled everyday to nearby Mohali where they worked in low-paid jobs as casual

labourers, petty vendors or factory hands. Few of the women
worked. Those who did were either domestic servants or
construction labourers. The Family Planning Association of
India, the NGO which took me to this slum, had a specific
agenda in view. They wanted to spread the message of family
planning in this area where most women had more than four
or five children.

Manjit Singh and his team from the FPAI had been here
many times before. Many of the women greeted them as we
walked past their huts. We went past a pool of stinking
stagnant water, through fly-ridden lanes, right into the heart
of the slum. About a dozen women were waiting for us.

They brought out their charpoys, collected a couple of
rickety chairs and offered us tea. Soon we were comfortably
seated, surrounded by the women and their children of various
ages, and of course the omnipresent flies.

Mahendra Kaur, the village midwife, who sat next to me,
seemed to be the most important person there. She herself
had three sons and a daughter. She spoke of the deliveries she
conducted using the most basic equipment and under these
unhygienic conditions. But she lost very few babies, she said
with pride. Boys or girls, these women just kept them. It was
a totally informal meeting. But, as I spoke to the women in
this semi-rural slum, I realized that they had no specific gender
preference not because they did not desire to have sons, but
because they actually had absolutely no control over the
number of children they produced. The children just
happened. They had no means to prevent them from being
born. Importantly, they had no 'traditional' way of
eliminating daughters, and no money for expensive sex
determination tests.

Lal Munni, for example, was a woman of indeterminate
age. She had five daughters and a son. The eldest daughter

was nine years old and the youngest was still suckling. She was an illiterate, disempowered woman eking out a living far away from where she was born. Her children played around in the slum and the only school they had been to was the free anganwadi. Sometimes parents did make an attempt to send their sons to school, one of the women said. However, the girls usually stayed home and looked after the younger siblings until they themselves got married.

'Anyone would prefer to have more sons,' one of the women remarked, 'but it is not in our hands.'

Sangeetha, a young woman in her twenties with a baby girl on her hip, said she had come to this place from her village in Bihar just a year ago. She said she was much happier here than she had ever been in her village, although she was still as poor as she had always been.

'But, I wish I had a son,' she joked. 'Then I could have bossed over my daughter-in-law like my husband's mother bossed over me.'

This set the women off. They spoke of the dowries they had brought from their natal homes. Of the way they were ill-treated by their in-laws.

'I wouldn't even get food to eat.'

'Even when I was expecting, I had to work in the fields.'

'I was kicked and beaten because my father did not give the cycle he promised.'

But, strangely their suffering had not made them reject their daughters. Struggling to live was such a part and parcel of their lives. Everyone struggled. Men and women alike. At that level, gender did not seem to matter. And so, at last, in a most unexpected corner of the country I had found a community which kept its daughters. Not that the families here actively wanted their daughters. They just had no means of rejecting them.

8

Backlash

In February 2006, Tripala Kumari, an eighteen-year-old tribal girl from Darhi village in Ranchi was killed by her husband Ajmer Singh, a farmer in Dohola village in the Jind district of Haryana.

Her crime? She refused to sleep with his brothers.

The tribal girl from Jharkhand district was brought to Haryana by an agent who promised to get her a job. She was 'married' to Ajmer Singh who desperately wanted a male heir. However, soon after her marriage she found she was expected to sleep with all his brothers. When she refused, he killed her.

The murder of Tripala Kumari gave a gruesome face to a form of sexual exploitation which was becoming increasingly popular in the women-starved states of Punjab and Haryana. The media had even given this kind of exploitation a name: The Draupadi Syndrome.

In the great Hindu epic the Mahabharata, which is set in this part of the country, Draupadi is a princess who is married to the five Pandava brothers. Arjuna the ace archer wins her hand in a tough competition. When he returns home and tells his mother Kunti that he has brought home a prize, she reacts by saying he should share it with all his brothers. Since Kunti's word is irrevocable, Draupadi ends up as the wife of all five brothers.

Today, Kurukshetra, the great battleground where the epic Mahabharata war was fought, is part of Haryana. In the 2001 census report it figured as one of the 'top ten districts with the lowest sex ratios' in the country. I knew the sex ratio was always low in this part of the country. But, was polyandry prevalent even at the time of the Mahabharata? If it was, why did the epic have to justify the marriage of Draupadi to five men?

In the present day context, another question was bothering me more. Was polyandry an unhappy tradition which had been discarded and then picked up again because of the alarming decline in the population of women? Some years ago, I had not heard of polyandrous marriages in Punjab. Was that because, like infanticide, fraternal polyandry was usually a well-kept family secret?

In Chandigarh, Dr S.K. Sandoo head of the Mohali Family Planning Association told me how she had stumbled upon the practice of polyandry in rural Punjab by sheer chance many years ago. Dr Sandoo, who was in her seventies in 2005, recalled how as a twenty-five-year-old she had camped in villages as part of her duties. It was then that she learnt that in some households the farmers shared a wife. Outsiders were led to believe that the younger brothers were not married because they did not want the property to be split. Dr Sandoo said that the farmers never admitted they shared a wife. They were vague about the paternity of the children. All the children were supposed to belong to the eldest brother who was the only one who was married to the woman of the household. The rest of the brothers were officially bachelors. So, wife sharing as a strategy to keep the landholding within the family seems to have existed in rural areas for quite some time. The woman famine had only given it an uglier and more exploitative turn.

The green revolution had turned Punjab into one of the most prosperous states. But it had also created two kinds of farmers. There were the rich farmers with large land holdings, vast properties and garages full of expensive cars, and there were the marginal farmers who managed to make a living on family holdings, which were viable only as long as they were not divided. Both varieties of farmers wanted only sons, because land could traditionally be passed on only from father to son.

This unquenchable thirst for sons had created a predominantly masculine society where women had become scarce commodities. The rich farmers because of their wealth could at least attract some girls from their own communities. The poorer ones had no alternative. They had to purchase women from poor tribal belts and other poverty stricken areas of Bihar and Orissa.

These 'bought' women were not really accepted either by the community or by the family. Such a wife's status even within the household was that of a domestic and sexual slave. As she was most often poor and illiterate and did not even know the language, she had no means of escape even if the situation was totally unpleasant. Some women committed suicide or tried to run away. Most of them endured their lives because they saw no viable alternative.

When an NGO in Punjab offered to take me to meet Rani, a tribal woman who was married to five Jat brothers, I did not think I would learn anything new. Polyandry was such a well-kept secret that most families denied it even existed. They might admit to buying women from 'outside', but not a single family had admitted that the woman was used by all the brothers. She was always just called the eldest brother's wife. Almost every family I visited claimed that the women were not exploited and that they enjoyed good lives. Often the women did not speak. But that, I was told, was because they did not have good command over Hindi.

Rani was different. She was slightly educated and could manage a conversation in Hindi. She was probably willing to speak to me because she had accepted her lot. She did not want me to identify either her village or her family. Her only concern was that since she had now reached a level of contentment, she did not want her boat rocked.

Rani had grown up in Jharkhand district and had attended a mission run school for a couple of years. When she was just fifteen, an agent had persuaded her father to sell her to a farmer from Punjab for Rs 50,000. Rani was a beautiful girl and so her father managed to get a better price than most other fathers. Her husband was thirty years old. Rani has never seen her father again. She has no idea what happened to the money that was used to purchase her body and soul. Other women from Rani's area had married Jat farmers and gone to Punjab, but since she had not spoken to any of them, she did not know what sort of life to expect.

For the first two months, Rani said, life was comfortable. Her husband and his brothers went out to work and she and her mother-in-law looked after the house and cooked food. Since she came from a 'lower' social background her mother-in-law did not let her perform puja and did not admit her into some parts of the house. She said she did not really mind this.

Within a month or two the pressure on her began to build up. She was continuously told by her mother-in-law that she had been bought so that she could produce male heirs for the household. Within a year, she gave birth to a healthy baby boy.

That's when the sexual exploitation began. Her husband told her she would now have to begin sleeping with his brothers. He was waiting for her to produce a son so that he could have an heir whose parenthood could be traced to him. Now, he said, she had to satisfy his brothers since he could not afford to buy wives for all of them. She tried appealing to her mother-in-law thinking that as a woman she would understand how difficult that would be. But her mother-in-law just ignored her pleas. It was only later on that Rani learnt that her husband and his brothers had different fathers. Fraternal polyandry had long been a 'tradition' in their family. The only difference was that her mother-in-law was also a Jat, not an Adivasi like her. Rani's youngest brother-in-law was just fourteen when she got married. He was just one year younger than her and now he was also one of her husbands.

Over the years, she became pregnant several times over by all the brothers. She was allowed to have one daughter. After that, every time she became pregnant, she was taken to the closest town for a scan. If the child in her womb was a daughter it would be aborted. Rani had realized by now that she had no power over any part of her body . . . let alone her womb.

When she spoke to me, Rani was thirty years old. Her mother-in-law was no more. Her experiences had ravaged her once beautiful face. She suckled her youngest son as she spoke to me. Her eldest son was fourteen years old and going to school. Her only daughter had turned twelve and had just attained puberty. Rani did not know what her daughter's fate was going to be.

'Maybe it won't be any different from mine,' she sighed. 'After all families like ours have to survive. We cannot afford too many wives and any quarrels over property. We have to hold on to our land.' Rani had internalized all the problems of her family and accepted her situation. She said her 'real' husband was a good man. He protected her and kept his brothers under control. She knew that if he threw her out she would have nowhere to go.

In an article on son preference in Punjab, Ravinder Kaur of the Institute for International Studies, Copenhagen wrote in 2005, 'Another implication of bride shortage is a "formal" excess of bachelors. I call it formal because although many of them remain legally unmarried, they may have sexual and emotional access to a wife of the household.'

Ravinder Kaur called this 'surreptitious fraternal polyandry in which one "wife" is shared by several brothers.' She also said that 'because polyandry is not socially acceptable, very rarely do families come out in the open about it.'[1]

The bought women lead isolated lives because they come from a different social background and often do not even speak the language. They might undergo a lot of mental and physical trauma is such situations, but they hardly ever complain to an 'outsider'. Social workers point out that since most of these marriages are neither registered nor properly solemnized, they do not break any specific laws. They cannot even be considered bigamous unless one of the offended parties lodges a proper complaint. The woman who is at the centre of it all is so powerless that she cannot think of any other way of life. Since the arrangement has the tacit support of the community, the authorities can do little about it.

By 2005, buying tribal brides or brides from other disempowered communities had become an accepted practice in the prosperous but woman-starved states across the country.

'The girls are very happy here,' Kanti Bhai Swaran Bhai Pathak told me. 'I have been in the business for seven years now. I have brought so many tribal brides for Patel and Choudhary grooms from this area. You go and talk to them and see. They are all happy.'

We were sitting in Kanti Bhai's tiny drawing room in a village in the middle of Mehsana district in Gujarat. According to the 2001 census, the sex ratio in this district was 752. Social activists however feared it was actually much lower. Kanti Bhai was a marriage broker with a difference. He specialized in getting tribal brides for the bride-hungry bachelors from the surrounding areas. At first he was hesitant to talk to me. Had he broken a law? Why was I interested in him? Finally, Bhanesh, the volunteer from Young Citizen of India, a local NGO who had fixed the meeting, convinced him he had nothing to fear. And once Kanti Bhai got talking, he was a fund of information.

Buying brides from tribal areas was not a new practice, he said. As far as he knew it was more than twenty-five years old. He said sex selection was traditionally acceptable in this part of the country and had existed long before the scan made its appearance. According to Kanti Bhai, the first tribal bride came to this area from Baruch. Apparently she was now well-integrated into her family. Her children were even accepted as Patels by the community.

As a teenager, Kanti Bhai knew the agent who had arranged that marriage. He was fascinated by the idea. He too wanted to get into the business of bringing a bride from far away to be married into this community. He didn't realize then that this would prove to be a lucrative business. In those days, he said, such marriages were rare. But today, for agents like Kanti Bhai, business was booming. As the local women disappeared, there was an increasing demand for Adivasi brides. Now a veteran, he scouted around for girls in many of the poorer districts of south Gujarat. He knew exactly where to go. The sex ratio in tribal areas he told me was good. The adivasis did not discriminate against women. They had different problems. Poverty and alcoholism had driven their communities to a brink. Some areas like Kathiawad, he said, were really bad and the families there were more than willing to sell their girls, hoping perhaps that they would enter better lives in their new homes.

When a Patel or Choudhary groom married a girl from his own community, he would often get a dowry and a grand wedding paid for by the bride's family. He would also get material goods like a house and car, a fridge, TV, furniture and kitchen equipment. The expenses for all this would be borne by the bride's family. But when he bought a girl through an agent, the situation was different.

Agents like Kanti Bhai collected a fee from the family of the prospective groom. This had to cover his living and travel expenses plus his brokerage fees. Once he located a poor family which was willing to get their daughter married, he started bargaining. Usually the price was fixed at around Rs 35,000 to Rs 40,000. The girl and her parents were brought from their village at the groom's expense. The marriage ceremony itself was usually very simple and basic. The whole deal would cost the groom about Rs 1 lakh. The girl would bring nothing with her and often the groom even had to buy her a sari to wear at the wedding.

Kanti Bhai seemed to be a good man. He himself had five daughters and a son and he said he tried his best to see that the girls whom he brought from so far away were happy in their marital homes. In his wanderings, he said he had also come across many 'fraud' agents who cheated both the parties. There were also agents who used the same girls several times over to fix marriages. After a few days the girls would disappear without a trace, often taking valuables with them.

In Sabarkhatta, Natu Bhai Ramji Bhai Barot told me about a case which had shaken the small town in which he lived. A local Patel had married a tribal girl and brought her home to live with him. Within a few weeks, she ran away taking with her Rs 50,000 worth of money and jewellery. The groom's family then registered a police complaint and the girl was caught. She confessed that she was part of a small gang which specialized in this particular activity. The gang consisted of a couple of girls and an agent. The agent would scout around and fix the 'marriage' for a price. The 'parents' would collect the money. The girl would move to her new husband's house and soon decamp with whatever she could lay her hands on. Sometimes the gullible groom would even give her some jewellery to wear and that would be an extra bonanza.

In September 2005, the Ahmedabad edition of the *Times of India*, carried a report about some tribal girls who hoodwinked the men who 'married' them. A number of unmarried men from the Patel community from Chansma taluk in Patan district in Gujarat paid Rs 50,000 each to an agent to get them adivasi brides. A Tata Sumo full of tribal girls drove up on the appointed day and the agent conducted an 'impromptu marriage' between the couples. He gave Rs 10,000 each to the parents of the girls and disappeared with the rest of the money. The next morning the new brides also vanished with the gold and silver ornaments they were wearing.

According to the report, an estimated 150 agents and subagents were 'bride trading' in Gujarat, using tribal girls from Khedbrahma, Chhota Udepur, Dahod and South Gujarat. Of these forty agents operated from Khedbrahma which was mainly populated by Bhil tribals.

Laloo Desai of Manay Kalyan Trust was quoted as saying, 'The going rate is Rs 60,000 for a tribal bride, Rs 80,000 for a non-tribal girl and over Rs 1 lakh for a labour class Patel girl in Kutch.' Desai also told the reporter that some agents cheated gullible clients by introducing married tribal girls as prospective brides. These girls were paid Rs 1000 to Rs 2000 for just posing as prospective brides. Many of these brides deserted their new husbands after a couple of weeks.

According to Ila Vakria of the Ahmedabad NGO Chetna, in Umeedpur village of Idar a boy reportedly committed suicide after two tribal girls bought for him and his brother dumped them. In Mehsana, Dhrupad Joshi of Young Citizen of India Charitable Trust told me about thirty-six-year-old Nitish Patel of Denap village in Mehsana who paid Rs 40,000 for a tribal girl. Within a few weeks she left him to marry another man from Rajkot for a fee. Nitish was about to buy a girl for his brother as well when this happened.

Ila Pathak, director of the Ahmedabad Women's Action Group (AWAG), was skeptical about the big issue being made of 'fraud' tribal marriages.

'In fact,' she said, 'most of the tribal girls who are bought are treated quite badly. They come from poor circumstances and have no means of escape.'

Prabhudas Easwardas Patel, President of the Anandpura Dairy who has seen quite a few such marriages also felt that the girls were ill-treated. 'The marriage is not a marriage in the real sense. These boys marry adivasi girls not because they want wives but because they want slaves,' he said. Social activists point out that 'buying' a girl is in itself an unacceptable act. She is hardly ever treated as an equal in her new home. Her circumstances rarely improve because of such a marriage.

Many of the women who have married into Patel households do not in fact reveal their actual background. In Upkal village, I met two such wives who both said they were Rajputs from south Gujarat. Both of them claimed to have integrated into their new families, though they did not speak too much.

Twenty-three-year-old Hansa Behn who was seven months pregnant with her first child had been married for three years. She said she was happier here than in her natal home and that she had even encouraged two of her sisters to marry Patel men. Twenty-four-year-old Manisha who had got married four years ago was nursing her son when I visited her. She was a bit more withdrawn. She told me her marriage had been fixed by her 'uncle' who was a road-building contractor. He travelled a lot on his work, she said and he had fixed quite a few marriages between Rajput girls from her area and Patel men from this district. I asked her if she was in touch with any of the women from her village who had married and come over here. She just silently shook her head. She didn't go out of the house much, she said in a whisper. The women were wary about speaking to strangers. They kept looking anxiously at the men folk from the family who supervised the conversations. Obviously they led isolated lives.

So were these marriages of convenience actually breaking down old caste barriers or were they spawning new exploitative situations?

'Let us be quite clear. These men have not married tribal girls because they want to give them a better life or because they want to break down caste barriers,' Ila Behn said. 'They are marrying them as a last resort because they cannot find women in their own community. Therefore they treat them also like purchased commodities.'

It seemed so ironic that the very men and women who were accused of treating the tribal girls like commodities were the ones who said they did not want daughters because they were afraid they might be ill-treated by their in-laws. They obviously felt that having a daughter was an expense but they did not mind spending money to buy brides for their sons. The reasoning behind this was simple. Whatever money they spent on a daughter was wasted because it went to another family. Purchasing a bride was like purchasing any other gadget which would enhance the family infrastructure. For the price that had been paid for them, these bought brides were expected to turn into household slaves and son-producing machines.

There was one more backlash in Gujarat. Thanks to the girl shortage a discarded system of marriage was making a come back. The *saata-paddhati* is a tradition followed by the Chowdhary, Rabari, Patel and Prajapati communities. According to this tradition, a girl is given in marriage only if the groom-to-be has a sister who can marry her brother. In other words the brother and sister from one family are married to the brother and sister of another family.

Ideal though it sounds, this tradition actually spawned many mismatches and disastrous matrimonial alliances. Deepika, a working woman living in Bangalore told me her own sad story. When she was in her mid twenties, her marriage had been arranged according to the saata tradition. She and her brother were married to a brother and sister.

'My brother and his wife were quite happy,' she said. 'He is well-educated and runs his own business in Ahmedabad. My sister-in-law has completed her schooling. She is very pretty and an excellent homemaker. Unfortunately, her brother and I were totally mismatched. He had just finished his schooling. I am a post-graduate. He is also five years younger than me and also shorter. We had nothing in common. My parents forced me into the marriage because they wanted my brother to get married. My brother is two years younger than me. They wanted him to marry. They wanted a girl from our community and they wanted him to have sons. In fact my marriage got postponed because they wanted to use me to get a good bride for my brother. My husband's family also wanted him to marry a Patel girl and since there is a shortage of girls in our community they forced him to marry me.'

Deepika's marriage was doomed from the start. She could not live with her husband for more than a couple of months. She was forced to stay married to him for several years because every time she tried to leave, her husband's family would threaten to make his sister leave her brother. When she finally walked out and found herself a job in Bangalore, her brother's marriage also collapsed. Deepika is now eaten up with guilt. Maybe she should have tried harder.

'A number of saata marriages collapse,' said Kala Bhai Dwarakdas Patel, husband of the Anandpur village sarpanch. 'And when one marriage fails it affects all the other marriages in the family. Like a house of cards. And it happens quite often because there are a lot of mismatches. In our community we discarded saata because of the problems. But, if the sex ratio keeps going down, we may have to reintroduce it. In that way each family will feel obliged to have a daughter so that they can exchange her for a bride for their son. '

Meanwhile in the dry desert belt of Rajasthan where the families have already finished off all their girls, there is a perennial girl drought. Here too, the *Aata-Saata* or 'double jodi' system as it is locally known was making a magnificent comeback. In Jhunjhunu, Churu and Sikar, nearly 30 per cent of the marriages conducted in 2005 were fixed under this 'swap' system. In some of these villages, the sex ratio was an abysmal 500 or less. So a family with a girl became much sought after. There was even a premium attached to some girls. An educated and beautiful girl was worth two plain and uneducated girls in this exchange market.

Dharmpal Chaudhary of Raghunathpura got his college-going daughter married to a family in the adjoining Indrapura village. In exchange, he got the two illiterate sisters of his new son-in-law as brides for his two sons.

The saata system had another advantage. Since there was a mutual exchange of girls, there was no dowry to be paid. So daughters were once more desired, but only as commodities to be used for exchange. Bizarre though it sounded, perhaps there was some truth in what Kala Bhai said. For families which had traditionally practiced saata, the disappearance of sisters had given the problem another dimension. Many men were forced to remain unmarried simply because they did not have a sister to exchange. The point was that though sisters had become desirable commodities, as far as their status was concerned, nothing had changed. They were still just commodities whose bodies were used as barter in a marriage transaction.

By reviving an undesirable tradition, could a desirable result be achieved in the long run? Did the means not matter if the end could be attained?

In Anandpur, during our session with the women, Dhrupad Joshi had said, 'The original Patels are getting destroyed. If you continue to kill off your girl children, you will have no women left. And when you want to get your sons married you will have to search for a Patel girl with a pair of binoculars! As it is many of you are going to tribal areas and buying girls for your sons. Soon the original Patel features would have disappeared. All your children will have adivasi features. Is it not ironic that you destroy your own daughters and go and buy daughters-in-law from somewhere else?'

It was a shocking and disturbing speech.

'You were shocked?' Joshi asked in a satisfied tone. 'Then I am pleased. My objective has been achieved. I want to shock these people so that they will stop doing what they are doing. All our goody-goody speeches have not worked. We have to really shock them into action now.' But I was shocked not by the fact that Patel children would have adivasi features. But by the fact that caste purity was being used as a strategy to curb female foeticide.

It was all so mixed up. On the one hand unborn girls were being slaughtered to 'protect' them from falling into impure hands. On the other, girls were being bought to continue the lineage. Daughters were a burden because they had to be expensively married off. Sisters were a necessity because without them brothers could not get married. What caste pride? What caste purity?

In Punjab because of the clamp down on sex determination clinics another discarded practice was rearing its ugly head. In June 2004, in an article titled 'Instant Injustice', Vijaya Pushkarna, the Chandigarh correspondent of *The Week* magazine wrote about a just-born female infant who was strangled by her mother in a hospital in Chandigarh.

'On a cold January night,' she wrote, 'the silence at the Post Graduate Institute in Chandigarh was pierced by the wails of a baby girl. Its mother Geeta sat by its side unmoved. After a while, she started hitting the newborn as if to stifle its cries. The commotion attracted the duty nurse who advised Geeta to feed the baby instead of thrashing it. Some time later, the baby stopped crying. The next day the nurse realized the secret behind the baby's silence. It had been strangled.'

Geeta confessed to the police that she had strangled her daughter because she could not afford another girl. Vijaya Pushkarna wrote about bodies of babies found in drains and rubbish dumps. She also quoted gynecologist Gurdeep Kaur who told her that because of the tightening of the laws, people were finding it difficult to get sex determination tests done and so they were either killing or abandoning their girl children. Female infanticide seemed to be making a comeback. Forced polyandry, purchasing women as sex slaves and household chattels, female infanticide ... could the status of women be worse?

9

The Ravaged Womb

When I floated inside my mother's womb, she used to play the veena. She has often described to me how as a sturdy eighteen-year-old, she would carry her heavy veena against her pregnant stomach and walk across to her teacher's house twice a week for her lessons. She continued to play until she could no longer sit on the floor and balance her veena against her stomach.

'I wanted to keep on playing as long as I could,' she would tell me, 'because I knew that those beautiful sounds would reach you. My grandmother told me that if you heard the sound of the veena from inside my womb, you would grow up to be a calm and gentle person. I knew that you were listening from inside me. I knew the music would somehow affect you in a positive way.'

That was more than half a century ago. Every time I hear her talk about it, I feel I can almost remember listening to that veena from inside her womb. But did I really 'hear'? And if I did, when did I start hearing it? When I was an eight-week-old foetus or an eight-month-old one?

Many, many years later, when I was pregnant with my children, I would listen to music all the time. Classical, pop, jazz, film, anything. I am not a musician myself, but I wanted them to experience those positive vibes of music too. Would they learn to love music as they lay floating, cherished and secure inside my womb? I really believed they would. I would eat all the right food for them. Carrots to make their eyes sharp and beautiful. Apples to make them healthy. Almonds to give them strength. Whenever I ate anything delicious, I would think it reached them as they lay inside me. When I smelt something good, I thought they could smell it too. I would croon to them when they kicked me and soothe them by stroking my stomach. Every little nuance, every little movement was a source of wonder. All my actions were focussed on keeping that little embryo growing inside my womb comfortable, strong and healthy. I knew it could never be harmed as long as it lay inside the safest place on earth . . . its mother's womb.

What about that foetus in my womb? Was it aware of me? Of how I felt about it? Was it aware that I was its mother? Did it feel safe inside my womb? Did it feel pain? Could it taste the food I ate? And if it did have any of these feelings, when did they begin to take shape?

Dr Arnold Gessell of Yale University spent a lifetime researching the behaviour of embryos. Way back in 1945, even before I was born, he wrote, 'By the close of the first trimester the foetus is a sentient, moving being. We need not speculate as to the nature of his psychic attributes, but we may assert that the organization of his psychosomatic self is well under way.'[1]

Foetal awareness has been a subject of intense political and academic debate. At what stage can a foetus feel pain? At what stage do its senses develop? When does it actually become a human being as we know it? Most scientists now believe that a foetus feels physical pain sometime during the pregnancy. But, when exactly does this happen? Within twelve weeks of conception . . . or much, much later?

The problem is the multiple nervous systems which are involved in the sensation of pain develop at different stages of gestation. Nociceptors, which are sensory receptors, appear as early as seven weeks post conception. The spinal column and the thalamus through which the signals pass are functional at about thirteen weeks. But the final necessary connections within the cerebral cortex, which interprets the signal as pain, are not developed until about the twenty-sixth week. Some neurologists feel that once the spino-thalamic system is fully developed, the foetus can feel pain. This happens at about twelve to fourteen weeks after gestation. To support their theory that a foetus at this stage can feel pain, they point out that it will withdraw from painful stimulation and that two types of stress hormone, which are detected in adults who are feeling pain, are also found in the blood sample of the foetus taken at this time.

As I delved into the issue of female foeticide, some new questions popped into my mind. The sex of a foetus can be detected only when it is between twelve to sixteen weeks old. A few weeks later the final connection to the brain is made. Can she feel pain after twelve weeks? Does she breathe? Can she move? Is the foetus, who is given the death sentence because her tiny genitalia have just become visible already 'a sentient, moving being whose psychosomatic self was well under way'?

Researchers have found that at nine weeks, the foetus's ballooning brain allows her to bend her body, hiccup, and react to loud sounds. At week ten, she can move her arms, 'breathe' amniotic fluid in and out, open her jaw, and stretch. By twelve weeks she can yawn, suck, and swallow, as well as feel and smell. By thirteen to fifteen weeks a foetus's taste buds already look like a mature adult's. Doctors know that the amniotic fluid that surrounds her smells and tastes strongly of the spices and other essences from a mother's diet. The thirteen-week-old foetus in her mother's womb can probably actually taste these flavours which, if she is allowed to live, will go on to become an intrinsic part of her life. Studies show that the foetal heart rate slows when the mother is speaking, suggesting that the foetus not only hears but also recognizes the sound and is calmed by it. Does the little one floating in her mother's amniotic fluid feel calm and safe even as her mother speaks about how she will eliminate her before she is born?

These thoughts are so bizarre. The womb which is supposed to be the safest place on earth has been desecrated and ravaged beyond recognition. It no longer belongs to the woman and her child. It belongs to a son-greedy society which has no qualms about tearing it open again and again and again. The ravaged womb is no longer a sanctuary for the unborn daughter. Nor is it any longer an intimate part of a woman's anatomy which belongs to her and her alone. Sex-selective abortion does not give women the right to choose. It only gives a misdirected society the right to selectively pluck innocent daughters from their mothers' wombs and massacre them. It is like a holocaust. Daughters have no place to hide any more because even the safest place on earth has been invaded.

In November 2005, a group of social workers from an NGO in Tamil Nadu were taking me around some villages where they had programmes to stop female infanticide. It was noon and we had just sat down in front of our banana leaves for lunch in a small rural hotel, when one of them got a call from home on her cell phone. Her ten-year-old son had been admitted in hospital. The woman just got up and rushed off without a word. Her colleagues continued with their meal. They looked sad, but not particularly worried.

'Poor thing,' one of them remarked, 'It happens quite often. She took some herbal medicine when she was pregnant. And that affected the child's health.'

'Why?' I asked. 'What was the medicine for?'

'Because she thought she was having a daughter and she wanted to abort the foetus,' she said. 'But she had a son. And he was born with a lot of health problems caused by the medicine. He is physically and mentally stunted and is always sick.'

The sad part of the story is that this woman had been working with an NGO to prevent female infanticide in the villages around Usilampatti for nearly fifteen years. Then why did she do this? Because her husband, who was unemployed and a wastrel, threatened to leave her if she didn't produce a son. But, ironically, the son she produced only widened the rift between them. He blamed her for everything that had happened and left the house whenever there was a crisis.

It didn't really shock me that a woman who was working to stop female infanticide should herself have wanted to abort a child when she thought it was female. By this time I had accepted the fact that sex-selective extermination is a great leveller. It knows no caste or creed, no socio-economic or language or educational barriers. Family pressures and the threat of being beaten or thrown out of the house overrides all sensitivities. Under such circumstances a woman values her own life above that of an unknown, unseen daughter. She willingly submits herself to the womb raiders. If she can afford it she has a scan. If she can't she goes to a quack. The poorest of the poor women get rid of their daughters after they are born.

In a small town near Madurai in Tamil Nadu, Dr Asha Devi, a gynaecologist, told me that more and more women were coming to her clinic with complications arising out of botched abortions. Due to the stricter laws, she said, the women found it increasingly difficult to get a sex-selective scan done on time. If they left it too late and the abortion became complicated they lost their babies as well as their physical and mental health.

'Perhaps they were better off killing the girl child after she was born,' an old midwife in Madurai remarked to me. 'Now their wombs are torn to pieces because they have so many operations to get rid of the child even before it is born.'

In 2005, the United Nations Fund for Population (UNFPA) published some gruesome findings from a study on sex selective abortions in Rajasthan. The study cited the case of Mrs Ravi who was a teacher in a public school. Her husband was a senior executive in a multinational. They had two daughters. In her quest for a son, Mrs Ravi underwent nine sex determination tests and had eight pregnancies medically terminated. She died two days after her son was born.

Ruhani Kaur, a Delhi-based photojournalist spent a year tracking female foeticide across the country. In 2006, she published the photograph of a badly deformed male child born to a village woman in Haryana. This woman who already had three daughters had taken some local 'medicine' in order to have a son. The medicine affected the child in her womb.

In Punjab and Haryana, almost every village, every town and every suburb had stories of women who died in the process of undergoing multiple abortions in order to have sons. Or of children who were born with birth defects because the mothers had taken some potion either to ensure a male child or to abort a female child. And yet it hadn't stopped. It was almost as if the women had a death wish for themselves and their never-to-be-born daughters.

The Medical Termination of Pregnancy (MTP) Act passed in 1971 guaranteed women in India the right to legally terminate an unintended pregnancy, provided it was done by a recognized medical practitioner in a government hospital or a place which had been approved by the government. Not all pregnancies could be terminated. There were some clear-cut guidelines.

And, since the MTP Act was supposed to help control India's exploding population, it had a rather unique feature. The failure of contraceptive device, irrespective of the method used (including natural methods) was also included as a reason for getting a legal MTP done. In fact all pregnancies could be terminated under this umbrella clause. The procedure for getting an MTP was also fairly simple. A woman over eighteen years of age had only to give her own written consent. It did not matter if she was married or single. Even her husband's consent was not required. A minor had to have her guardian's consent.

Therefore, for a first trimester abortion, the procedure was very simple. It could be done on the advice of a single authorized practitioner. When the pregnancy exceeded twelve weeks but was below twenty weeks, the opinion of two registered practitioners was necessary.

The MTP Act was supposed to bring down the maternal mortality rate by curbing illegal and unsafe abortions. However, twenty-five years after it was passed the number of such abortions continued to be as high as before. The complications arising from unsafe abortions continued to claim the lives of hundreds of women across the country. Since there were no proper records, those working in the field could only rely on 'guesstimates'. According to some analysts, for every one woman who went for a legal abortion there were more than ten who had illegal ones.

The reason was simple. Women did not go in for abortions because they wanted to limit their families. Very few had an abortion for health reasons. For most women, an abortion had evolved into a planned strategy. Every abortion had to be made 'worthwhile' by ensuring that a baby of the wrong sex was not born.

In this scenario, first trimester abortions were not feasible. Since the genitals of the foetus were visible only towards the tail end of the first trimester, all sex-selective abortions had to be done only in the second trimester. Although second trimester abortions were also allowed under certain stricter conditions, obviously the women who wanted to do it for the purpose of sex selection would prefer not to go in for a legal MTP.

A Gujarati proverb goes: 'Having a hundred deliveries is better than having a single miscarriage.' Having an induced sex-selective abortion in the second trimester is probably much, much worse even than having a miscarriage.

A miscarriage is caused by natural problems which force a usually dead foetus out of the womb. A foetus which is aborted is usually healthy, and has to be either plucked or sucked out forcefully or artificially ejected from the womb. In any case the womb in which it once grew gets a bad beating. Over the 100 potential physical complications associated with abortion, some are immediately apparent while others reveal themselves days, months or even years later.

A second trimester abortion can be performed in several ways. The most commonly used method probably is the good old D&C or Dilation and Curettage. For this the cervix is dilated or stretched to insert a loop-shaped steel knife. The body of the foetus is cut up and removed from the placenta. If this procedure is done by an inexperienced person there is a high risk of excess bleeding, uterine perforation and infection. In another procedure called Suction Curettage or Vacuum Aspiration, the cervix is progressively dilated and the foetus is sucked out with a vacuum machine or syringe. The most frequent post-abortion complications occur with this method. If any foetal or placental tissue is left behind in the uterus, infections can develop. If any of these procedures are done by a careless or inexperienced medical practitioner, there are chances of the woman ending up with a perforated uterus or bladder or even bowel. If all the 'products of conception' are not extracted, severe infection can set in.

By 2006, a medical abortion had become the most popular option. It was less messy. The woman did not have to get admitted for more than a day. And more importantly, there was no need for a sterile operation theatre and instruments. However, what most women did not realize was that this seemingly harmless procedure carried its own set of risks.

Using Ethacradine Acetate for example is pretty simple. It can be introduced through a sterile catheter into the uterus and placed behind the pregnancy sac. This painless procedure can cause an abortion within two to three days. The procedure is safe, cheap and easily available. To hasten the process, prostaglandin or oxytocin is also injected. But, unless this is monitored carefully, the uterus can rupture. And, if the medical practitioner is not skilled, the uterus can be damaged by the catheter.

An even simpler procedure is to insert a gel of prostaglandin called Cerviprime into the mouth of the uterus in the evening in the clinic. The woman can go home for the night. Early the following morning in the hospital she is given a drip of oxytocin and within twenty-four hours she aborts. This too, unless carefully monitored can cause a ruptured uterus.

The most favoured and least messy method of abortion

perhaps is to induce labour by giving the woman tablets of Mifepristone or RU-486, a drug which was approved in France in 1988. This became available in India by 2000. RU-486 interrupts pregnancy by blocking the action of the natural hormone progesterone, which prepares the lining of the uterus for the fertilized egg. The progesterone retains and sustains the pregnancy. Once the effect of this is removed, the foetus stops growing and dies. The result is similar to a naturally occurring miscarriage. Common side effects from the use of this tablet are cramps and abdominal pain, nausea and vomiting, diarrhoea and uterine bleeding. If the abortion is not successful, women has to have a surgical abortion to complete the process. The Mifepristone has to be followed by a vaginal dose of Misoprostol which the woman can insert herself. The uterus then contracts causing cramping and the foetus is ejected. The cramps and the bleeding stop only after the dead foetus comes out.

According to FDA guidelines in the US, Mifepristone can be used only within forty-nine days of the beginning of the woman's last menstrual period. The FDA allows Mifepristone to be distributed only to doctors trained to accurately diagnose the duration of the pregnancy and to detect ectopic or tubal pregnancies in which case the drug cannot be used. It has restricted Mifepristone's use to doctors who can operate in case a surgical abortion is needed on a follow-up visit or in cases of severe bleeding.

The problem with all these extremely 'simple' procedures is that unless they are carefully monitored, the woman can haemorrhage and her uterus can rupture. The amount of bleeding when using Mifepristone is greater than with surgical abortion. As in surgical abortion, here too foetal matter can get left behind in the uterus and cause septic infections.

In 2004, Dr S.G. Kabra petitioned the Rajasthan State

Human Rights Commission to stop the across-the-counter sales of Mifepristone. He pointed out that according to the MTP Act, the termination of a pregnancy could only be done under stipulated conditions in approved centres and by approved doctors. Therefore, he said, this drug which induced abortion should be sold only to qualified medical practitioners and that the termination of the pregnancy should take place only in a hospital or recognized centre, which had all the required facilities including provisions for giving blood transfusions.

Dr Kabra pointed out that since the drug was being freely sold across the counter, anybody could buy it and give it to pregnant women. Due to this, he said, in the rural areas, many women had died of excessive bleeding or other complications.

The commission ruled in his favour. This did not mean that pharmacists stopped selling Mifepristone over the counter. Like in the case of any other similarly prohibited drug, the friendly neighborhood pharmacist was still willing to bend the rules. Sometimes he made a bit of money by charging extra for the 'risk' he was taking.

'Why talk about corrupt pharmacists,' a leading gynaecologist in Bangalore demanded angrily. 'I know many of my colleagues who keep the tablets in their clinics and sell them to their patients at a higher cost. If it costs Rs 900 in the medical shop, they sell it in their clinics for Rs 2000.'

By 2006, the relationship between many doctors and their patients had somehow morphed into medical service provider and client. Viewed from that perspective, the client who came for a sex-selective abortion struck a pure business deal with the service provider who gave her the 'package'. There was no personal involvement. The service provider was only concerned about not getting caught because of a botched abortion or some other similar slip-up. The client's actual long-term health was not a real concern. The clients who were usually quite ignorant about the possible health consequences just plunged into the deal driven by social forces beyond their control. And as usual, advanced technology only spelt greater doom for the daughters with nowhere left to hide.

10

Yesterday, Today, Tomorrow

In 1981, I met Marianne Lindstorm, a journalist from the Swedish Broadcasting Corporation who came to Trivandrum following up a frail link wrought in the nineteenth century between Sweden and Kerala.

The link in question was a novel written nearly a 100 years before by an Indologist named C.J.L. Almqvist. The heroine of the novel, a glazier's daughter who inherits her father's business, lays down ten conditions before she marries the man she loves. The main condition is that she would continue to live her own life in her natal home and her husband could have a 'visiting' relationship with her.

Almqvist was a widely read man who drew his inspiration from accounts of the Malabar coast written by early travellers. His novel, which was considered very radical, was severely criticized in Sweden when it was published. Even though they outnumbered men, the status of women was particularly low in nineteenth century Sweden. They had no economic independence as most jobs were denied to them because of their gender. Therefore, to them, the idea of women owning property and having the freedom to change sexual partners was almost inconceivable.

Feminists in Sweden believed that, though Almqvist had not mentioned Kerala anywhere in his book, the idea of a visiting husband could have been inspired by the *sambandam* system of marriage which prevailed among the Nairs of Kerala in the nineteenth century.

Sambandam was an off-shoot of *marumakkathayam*, the matrilineal tradition of the Nairs who were the dominant Hindu community of Kerala. Quite a few Hindu communities in this southwestern-most tip of India lived in matrilineal households in the nineteenth century, when this Swedish novel was written. Their social mores were quite different from the rest of patriarchal India. The most important difference was that unlike the patriarchal families, these matrilineal families considered women to be an economic asset.

The traditional Nair *marumakkathayam* family, called a *tharavadu*, consisted of the women and men who were born into that family. The children belonged to the mother and were brought up in her natal family. The eldest male of the family, who was called the *Karanavan*, exercised full powers over the affairs of the joint family. Women never left their natal home even after they were married. *Sambandam* marriages were generally arranged by the *karanavan* and the ceremony itself was an extremely simple one. The husband would not live permanently with his wife but would visit her for periods of time and then return to his own *tharavadu*. The children would stay with their mother. A *sambandam* relationship could be terminated by either of the partners and both of them were free to enter new relatiosnhips.

The link between the 'sambandam' type of marriage existing among the Nairs of Kerala in the nineteenth century and Almqvist's 'visiting husband' was pointed out by Vastman-Berg, a feminist scholar who wrote a thesis on the subject in the 1970s.

However, in the 100 years that had passed since the novel

was written, things had changed dramatically. Swedish women were no longer subservient. They were independent and held well-paid jobs. The institution of marriage had taken a battering and now women had learnt to live on their own outside its confines.

In the 1970s, in Kerala, for women in the matrilineal households, things had changed too, but not necessarily for the better. The matrilineal family which had given them a certain status and independence no longer existed. The *sambandam* system of marriage had vanished almost without a trace. The women of Kerala were now bound into the traditional marriage, which in India meant they did not inherit property but paid dowry. No jobs were barred to them because of their gender. However, most women opted to go for traditionally 'feminine' jobs like teaching or nursing.

In the 1980s, Kerala society was in a state of transition. The nuclear family was seen as the ideal family set up and the visiting husband system of marriage was viewed as an embarrassing tradition which was best forgotten. Not many were willing to talk about life in the *tharavadus* and Marianne Lindstorm, most probably returned home disappointed.

There was not much literature available on the *tharavadus*. For, though many researchers had published work on the adverse effects of patriarchy not too many had looked at the positive impact of a matrilineal system on women who lived within it. So, no one knew if there really was a link between Kerala's excellent sex ratio and the *marumakkathayam* families.

Marumakkathayam was a legal right which determined inheritance through the female line. Under this system, if a family property had to be partitioned all the female members would receive one share each. This meant that a woman, her children and grandchildren by her daughters would each receive a share. For the men, only those who were born into the tharavadu would get a share. Sons were not entitled to any share in the father's property. Since the heirs to the property were the women in the family and the menfolk were only allowed to enjoy the benefits during their lifetime, in a Nair *tharavadu* daughters were more important than sons.

Nair women lost this very important right to inherit property when the Kerala Joint Hindu Family System (Abolition) Act was passed in 1975. Once this happened, they became as devalued as women elsewhere. The Nair joint family, like joint families all over the country, collapsed due its own intrinsic deficiencies.

Historians differ on how the matrilineal *tharavadus* came into being. One of the theories is that since the Nairs were a martial race, the men were always on the move, leaving the women and their property unprotected. By creating these matrilineal homes, they ensured the safety of their women and children as well as their property. The men could also form relationships which were not necessarily binding for a life time, and they did not have to worry about the future of the children who were produced from such a liaison.

The women would only enter into *sambandam* relationships with persons of their own or higher castes as dictated by the eldest male member of the family. All the children belonged to the family and often they had no close relationship with their birth fathers. Since the *karanavan* was actually in charge, the women seldom had a say in the use or disposal of the property. Even marriages were fixed and dissolved by the *karanavan*. The women living in the *tharavadus*, therefore, did not enjoy the kind of sexual and economic freedom which the Swedish women thought they did. So, when the men decided to dissolve these unique joint families, the women did not really have a say.

The foundations of these *tharavadus* began to shake with the entry of the British. Like the nineteenth century Swedes, the British were shocked by the *marumakkathayam* system and the 'immoral' *sambandam* relationships.

Over the years, fewer wars were being fought and the Nair men had begun to settle down to sedentary lives. As more and more men got educated, they found non-martial job opportunities far from home. They were no longer dependent on their ancestral property for survival. Soon the men wanted to have nuclear families who could travel with them. Since the women who lived in the *tharavadus* were not equipped to hold jobs on their own, they became economic dependents. Thus began the process of what sociologist D. Renjini has called 'housewifization'.

Over a period of time, the men living in the *tharavadus* began to see the advantages of scrapping a decaying system which did not give them full control over property or inheritance. It did not take much to convince them that the entire social system was immoral and undesirable. As for the women, since they had never had any real control over their own affairs, they did not protest in any significant way when their right to inherit was taken away from them. Little did they realize then that this would strike the first death knell for future generations of unborn daughters in their community.

In December 2005, four scholars, S. Sudha, S. Khanna, S. Irudaya Rajan and Roma Srivastava, presented a paper entitled 'Traditions in transformation: Gender bias among the Nairs of Kerala', at a seminar on female deficit in Asia which was held in Singapore. They analysed the impact of modernization on the Nair women who belonged to a matrilineal society and tried to 'trace the origin of gender bias in a society which was once considered gender-egalitarian'.

By the end of the study, they had documented 'the emergence of substantial verbal gender bias and the limited use of pre-natal sex selection technologies to actualize this bias, in the Nair community'.

Women living under the matrilineal system, they pointed out, had some very distinct advantages. They had a comparatively high status within the family. They had strong inalienable rights within the *tharavadu*, which ensured them life long security and shelter. Widows and divorcees could remarry and women could terminate an unsatisfactory relationship. They also pointed out that since female veiling and seclusion did not exist, women went out of their homes to get educated.

Since the women inherited property, they did not pay dowry. But, most importantly since matrilineal descent highlights the female line, daughters were key members of the household. Though women did not usually have personal autonomy in the *tharavadus*, 'the birth of a daughter was never a disappointment, and there was no structural basis to consider daughters as liabilities'. So, they pointed out, a shift away from this system had profound negative implications on a woman's position both within the family and in society.

The matrilineal Nair families formed just a part of the Kerala mosaic. The patriarchal Namboodiri Brahmins, Christians and Muslims formed nearly 50 per cent of the population. However, since this part of the country was quite cut off from the rest of India, each community preserved some of its own social mores. Muslim women for instance were never veiled or secluded. Christian women practiced birth control. But, unlike the matrilineal Nairs, the women in these communities traditionally never inherited property.

Yet, in the 1980s, to the outsider, Kerala still seemed to be the most woman friendly state in the country. According to the 1981 census, the sex ratio was 1032, which was way above the national average. The death rate for women in Kerala was lower than for men. The birth rate was coming down. The average age of marriage for women was twenty-one. Female literacy was the highest in the country.

In fact the concept of family planning had been introduced to Kerala long before it was known in other parts of the country. In the 1930s, Maharani Sethu Parvathi Bai, the enlightened Maharani of Travancore, had invited Margaret Sanger, the family planning crusader, to Trivandrum to address a conference on birth control. At that time, the Christian women in the city protested. By the 1980s, however, family planning had been accepted by people belonging to all the religious communities.

In the 1970s, the number of women students studying in engineering colleges had gone up three fold. More women than men enrolled for post-graduate engineering courses in the state. About 250 women graduated every year from the medical colleges. Girls went to school and college even in the remotest corners of the state.

More women in Kerala went out to work. 38 per cent of the women were employed in factories as against 8.6 per cent which was the all-India figure. Kerala supplied the country with 75 per cent of its nurses and 90 per cent of its female circus artistes. Women athletes like P.T. Usha and Shiny Abraham were blazing trails across the country and the world. But even while all this was happening, those who lived in Kerala could see the cracks beginning to form.

In 1970, when I went to live in Kerala, I was an outsider wearing rose-tinted glasses. I thought I was landing in a part of the world where women were not second-class citizens. The mirage began to shake in an alarming manner on one of my very first journalistic assignments. I was commissioned to write an article, 'Nurses and Nuns of Kerala', for a government of India publication which came out in 1975 during the International Women's Year.

The nurses of Kerala were legendary. They were found in hospitals across the country and in some of the remotest corners of the earth. They endured tremendous hardships and often travelled alone. What gave them that courage and independence? Was it the matrilineal society? That's when I came across my first paradox.

Most of the nurses from Kerala were Christians who had never lived in a matrilineal family. They endured great hardship and danger not because they wanted economic independence, but because they were saving up money to pay dowries. They often came from poor or middle-class families and wanted to get themselves 'good' husbands through arranged marriages. They totally believed that it was the duty of women to pay dowry and they could not imagine getting married in any other way.

As I probed deeper, I realized that dowry permeated almost every aspect of a woman's life in Kerala as much as in any other part of the country. Even the nuns paid dowry to the church when they took their vows. Priests did not. Muslim girls in Malabar were sold off as brides to visiting Arab sheikhs because their parents did not have money to pay their dowries. On paper, local Muslim men paid a bride price. But in reality, the Muslim girls in Kerala like in other parts of the country paid dowry when they married local Muslim men. As for the Nair women, the old *tharavadus* had collapsed. By the 1970s, from owners of property they had become payers of dowry.

In local parlance dowry was called 'share'. Among the Christians, the dowry rates were much higher. Since Christian women never inherited ancestral property, the grooms-to-be demanded a good 'share', which was supposed to be equivalent to what the brothers would get.

In spite of this, Kerala, like the rest of south India, was still daughter-friendly.

In Punjab, by 1979, the first sex determination clinic had opened and already families were trying to selectively abort their female children. Punjab, of course, had a historical deficit of women and the New Reproductive Technologies (NRTs) coming in only aggravated an already bad situation. The census figures indicate that even as far back as 1901, the sex ratio in most of north India was less than the all India average of 972 females to 1000 males. During the same period in the south the sex ratios were well above the national average.

By 1981, Tamil Nadu was already sliding towards becoming a woman deficit state. The sex ratio in Kerala had also gone down to 1032, but it was still way ahead of the other states.

By 1991, demographers were beginning to sound the alarm about the daughters who were never born. And in its wake came some new questions. Why was the incidence of sex specific abortions higher in the northern and western parts of India? Amartya Sen raised this question once more in his typical poetic manner. 'The remarkable division of India (splitting the country into two disparate halves),' he said, 'is particularly puzzling. Are there differences in traditional cultural values that are hidden away?'[1]

Perhaps there were. The organization of families and marriage patterns in the south were very different from the north. Kerala of course had its own unique system. But in the contiguous areas of Tamil Nadu, Karnataka and Andhra Pradesh, families were like small clans. They married within themselves or within their own small communities.

In Tamil Nadu for instance there was the concept of *morrai* (by traditional right) *mapillai* (groom) or *penn* (bride). A girl's mother's brother or her father's sister's son was usually considered the person with the traditional right to marry her. This meant girls stayed within the family. There was no question of dowry being exchanged and since the girl's mother-in-law was her aunt or grandmother, relationships were easy. Unlike the north, where caring for a daughter was compared to watering a neighbour's plant, here daughters stayed in the family and were considered assets.

Karnataka, Andhra Pradesh and Kerala had similar traditions. The system of course had its own problems. Such blood-related marriages, which are called consanguineous, multiplied the chances of genetic diseases being passed onto the offspring. They also resulted in many unhappy mismatched marriages that took place just because a certain groom was bound by tradition to marry a certain bride. Individual choice did not come into the picture. The only social advantage was that girls kept their ties with their natal families.

Originally, dowry did not pay a big part while arranging a marriage in the south. Many communities had the custom of giving *stree dhanam*, which was essentially a gift given to the girl by her parents to help her set up a new home. If for some reason the marriage did not work out and she had to return to her parental home, she had a right to take her *stree dhanam* back with her.

Like north India, south India had its share of wars and invaders. But in the south, they tackled the problems in different ways. For example, while the soldiers of Punjab and Rajasthan preferred to kill off their women and girl children in order to protect them, in Kerala the warrior Nairs built safe homes for them. However, after independence, as India became one cohesive whole, some uniform social mores became acceptable across the length and breadth of the country. Some individual traditions survived, but many fell along the way.

Unfortunately, there was one particularly undesirable social more which not only survived, but also flourished and spread its tentacles right across the social spectrum. Dowry. *Dahej*. *Varudakshinai*. Call it by any name. It had always existed in a small way in most communities. But, post-Independence, it mutated into something quite different.

Dowry was no longer a gift of love given by the parents when a daughter set out for her new home. It had morphed into an evil which ruined families and took the lives of the very girls it was supposed to benefit. Dowry totally vilified the atmosphere cutting through all socio-economic barriers and oozing its way into communities which never even knew it existed. In the Great Indian Marriage Market, dowry created an insurmountable gender inequality. The market economics here were very simple. Boys were assets because they brought in money. Girls were liabilities because they took it away. Like all good business people, families wanted more assets. Even though they might have had some sentimental attachment to their liabilities, they would prefer not to have them at all.

As if in answer to their prayers, in the 1970s, the New Reproductive Technologies (NRT) came on to the scene. NRTs were like magic wands which could make wishes come true. In the beginning, the impact of these technologies was only felt in the already daughter-hostile belt. The 2001 census, however, threw up some new disturbing trends. Tamil Nadu was no longer in the 'safe' belt. It already had some districts with the lowest sex ratios in the country. In Karnataka, the alarm bells were sounding loud and clear. In Andhra, the child sex ratios were dropping fast in urban areas like Hyderabad where medical facilities were good. Most shockingly, the tremors could be felt even in Kerala.

In 2005, *The Kerala State Economic Review* came up with some findings which made demographers sit up and take notice of these tremors. The survey had found that although the overall sex ratio of Kerala was still good at 1058 females per 1000 males, the enrolment of girls in schools had been steadily declining over the years.

On an average, the number of girls joining schools was declining every year. The number of girls at the lower primary level, for instance, decreased from 9.15 lakhs in the academic year 2002-2003 to 9.05 in 2003-2004. By the next year it had come down to just 9 lakhs.

There was more disturbing news. A study conducted by the Achutha Menon Centre for Health Studies indicated that about 25,000 female infanticides occurred in the state in a year. To add to the problems, the Registrar General of India (RGI) said that the Infant Mortality Rate (IMR) for females had gone up while the IMR for males had gone down.

Kerala has had the lowest IMR in the country for forty years. While the IMR was 60 per 1000 in other parts of the country, in Kerala it was just 11. But the new data from the RGI revealed that the IMR for females was 12 per 1000 while the IMR for males had gone down to 8 per 1000. Which meant that even in woman-friendly Kerala many more female than male infants were dying.

Meanwhile studies were beginning to show that the disintegration of the matrilineal *tharavadus* had certainly had an adverse impact on the women. One study even found that in Kerala the greatest gender disparity was found among the Nairs. But, was there really cause for alarm? The child sex ratio at 963 was not bad compared to the national figure of 927. So where was the problem?

By now I had got used to seeing the huge problems in the

female deficit states. The problems there were obvious. They struck you in the face. I found it difficult now to focus on the details, which showed up the cracks that were beginning to appear on Kerala's women-friendly façade. It was a kind of progression. Every time I delved into a hidden crime against daughters, it was like opening a Pandora's box. The repercussions were enormous and the ripples kept moving further and further out. What seemed a mind-boggling and unbelievable crime at first faded before something more 'progressive'.

I started off with the medieval sounding crime of female infanticide. At that time, I could not imagine anything worse than a mother killing her own just-born daughter. But, as I went on, I realized that female infanticide, though uglier to view, faded into insignificance before the much more widespread crime of female foeticide.

Once upon a time the daughter in the womb was safe because her sex was unpredictable. There were pockets across the country where she was killed as soon as she was born. But they remained just that. Isolated pockets. Because killing a living, breathing little girl was not easy either on the heart or on the soul.

However, with the New Reproductive Technologies, hearts and souls did not come into the picture. Female foeticide became a high-tech crime. It was so unmessy. So easy. Sex detection techniques progressively became better and better. Abortion became easier and easier. Suddenly the womb became the most unsafe place on earth for daughters. Once more, the ripples started spreading in an alarming manner.

As for the medical fraternity which facilitated this process, sex-selective abortion was literally the goose that laid the golden egg. It was so lucrative that hearts, souls and medical ethics were just thrown to the winds.

By 2000, female foeticide had almost become a national pastime. But there were some safe havens. Some pockets of sanity. Or so we thought. By 2006, I knew that the fissures were appearing there too. By now I knew what to look for. And when I looked, I was terrified.

All the parameters were in place. Widespread medical facilities, high female literacy, prosperity, dowries which soared by the day, weddings which grew more and more ostentatious every year. It was just a question of time before the south went the way of the north. Was there any way it could be stopped? Some miracle formula? Some magic wand? Some wonderful empowering programme?

In Usilampatti, female infanticide was tackled by educating the women, empowering them with jobs and giving monetary benefits to those who kept their daughters. It had taken twenty years to have some effect. I would be naïve to imagine such a strategy would work on a national scale.

But, maybe it could work at some levels. At the very bottom of the pile where survival was an issue, attaching a monetary benefit to girl children might encourage families to keep them.

What about the doctors? The irony was that wherever medical facilities were widespread, female foeticide had raised its head. Sex-selective abortion was big, big, business. But, surely, all doctors could not be conspiring to cull female foetuses?

Doctors were highly educated human beings. They were trained to heal not kill. Obviously some kind of mutation had taken place. Could it be reversed? Could doctors across the country be sensitized in a more systematic manner? Maybe, if the medical fraternity realized the enormity of what was happening, they would apply peer pressure to weed out the corrupt. Maybe if enlightened doctors played a proactive role in preventing female foeticide they could turn the tide.

What about the educated women? All the studies had shown that educated women strategized better and eliminated their daughters more efficiently. So, was educating women working against their own gender? Were these educated women not given the right values? Obviously, the low self-esteem which women had internalized over generations could not be removed by conventional literacy. Without social and economic empowerment, education only rubbed salt into the wounds. It gave women one more reason to justify their existing low self-esteem.

Education itself was often seen only as a passport to a better marriage. I come from a family where women have been educated for generations. When my paternal grandmother got a BA degree in the early 1920s she became one of the earliest women graduates from Madras University. By the time she graduated, she was barely twenty and already the mother of two. But she never held a paid job because she never 'had' to.

Even in my generation, women were educated not so that they could be economically independent but because a college degree would enhance a girl's value in the 'marriage market'. Men preferred educated wives not only because they could move easily in their social circles but also because they could take care of all the 'outside' work like paying the bills, doing the grocery shopping, taking care of the day to day problems of the kids' school and homework.

A friend's husband would often proudly say, 'My wife has a post-graduate degree in maths, so she can help the kids with their homework. I don't have to hire a tuition teacher. Why does she have to go out to work? We don't need that extra money and she has enough to do at home.'

Yet, my friend was constantly conscious of the fact that

she was considered an economic liability. One of her husband's conditions had been that she should be a full-time mother and housewife. But every day he pointed out to her that she only 'spent' and never 'earned'. Her parents had paid through their noses to get her a husband who was better qualified than her. His parents had demanded a fat dowry and a house in the city because they had sent him abroad for his education. Their argument was that they had to be compensated for the money they spent on their son because his wife would get the full monetary benefit of the education which they had paid for.

Women in middle-class families were never expected to hold 'outside' jobs after they were married. A woman's place was at home tending the family. Only women who 'needed' the money for survival were 'allowed' to work.

In parts of the country where women from middle-class families did go out to work, ironically, better educated girls ended up paying bigger dowries. A 'discount' would be given only if she actually held a well-paid job.

When S. Sudha et al interviewed the Nairs of Thrissur, a young unmarried man of a lower economic status told them, 'Highly educated women will select highly qualified men. Then high dowry has to be given.'

A fifty-eight-year-old working woman of high socio-economic status echoed this sentiment saying a highly educated girl would not get any dowry 'discount'. On the other hand, 'She may have to give more. Because if she is highly educated, then she can only marry an educated man . . . and she has to pay high dowry. That is happening in all communities including Nairs,' she said.

The study concluded that dowry given at marriage emphasized the bride's family's inferior status. Grooms of course never paid dowry, no matter how highly educated or well employed the bride might be.

The marriage ads in the papers, in a way, said it all. Every groom-to-be wanted a fair, good-looking, educated, homely (read 'willing to be a full time home-maker') girl from a 'decent' (read 'able to pay dowry') family. If he himself came from a 'high status' family, it meant he expected extra perks like a grand wedding and a house and a car. Most families found nothing wrong with such aspirations. They had no doubt that women were economic liabilities and hence they had to pay to get accepted by a man's family. This widespread belief that women were inferior had become ingrained in men and women alike across the country.

If a man paid to get himself a wife, he bought a chattel; a slave. If a woman paid to get herself a husband, she was buying her way into a relationship in which she remained inferior. It was a no-win situation.

I came to the sad conclusion that no amount of legislation could take this away. Social boycott would not happen in any significant manner as long as society endorsed dowry. And dowry would not disappear as long as families believed that a woman was not as economically important to a family as a man. Obviously, women need a major image make-over.

Society needs to accept them as vital members of a family unit. Not as dowry-bringers. Or as son-bearing machines. More importantly, women need to believe in themselves. For, unless they do, their daughters will continue to die as unwanted foetuses.

But, when will this happen?

It should have happened yesterday.

It ought to happen today.

Because tomorrow may just be too late . . .

Afterword

Myth and Reality

Myth: As more female foetuses are aborted, women will become scarce and hence will be more valued and respected.
Reality: As women become scarcer, they become more devalued. Forced polyandry, kidnap and higher incidences of rape are a few of the unsavoury consequences.

Myth: When the deficit of girls reaches a critical level, society will spring back on its own. Daughters will be desired and sex ratios will become normal.
Reality: Female foeticide has resulted in an unnatural deficit of women. If it is not stopped, a couple of generations of women will be lost. With every new generation the number of women is decreasing in an alarming manner. The critical level may be crossed before society even comes up with a strategy to stem the depletion.

Myth: Only uneducated and poor families abort their female foetuses.
Reality: Studies have shown that educated parents 'strategize' better and that they are the ones who go in for sex-selective abortions. Poor parents cannot afford to buy the 'package' offered by the doctors.

Myth: Most families cannot 'afford' girls because they are expensive to bring up and the family incurs crippling expenses when they have to be married off.

Reality: Families incur an equal amount of expenditure on rearing boys. They spend more money on a boy's education, entertainment expenses and expensive toys.

Myth: Since society has turned evil and vulnerable girls have to be protected it is better not to have them at all.

Reality: This is like saying noise pollution is high and people who are sensitive to noise might get headaches, so cut off their heads!

Myth: Nurturing a girl is like watering a neighbour's plant. She is no use to the family after she gets married. Educating a son is like buying insurance for one's old age.

Reality: Girls are generally more attached to their parents and are more likely to look after them in their old age. The English proverb goes: 'A son is a son till he gets him a wife. A daughter is a daughter all her life'.

Myth: Doctors should not be persecuted. They are only fulfilling the wish of their clients to have sons.

Reality: Doctors are supposed to be healers and saviours of life. They are fully aware of the social and medical consequences of repeated sex-selective abortions. They are socially and legally obliged not to reveal the sex of the child to their clients.

Myth: Since abortion as a family planning strategy is legal in India, most families and many doctors do not know that sex-selective abortion is illegal.

Reality: All families and all doctors are aware of the difference between an ordinary abortion which is legal and a second trimester sex-selective abortion which is illegal.

Myth: A sex-selective abortion empowers a woman as she can have children of the gender of her choice and need not go through multiple unwanted pregnancies.
Reality: A sex-selective abortion shows up the ultimate powerlessness of a woman who has no control even over the foetus she bears in her own womb. Social and familial pressures force her to subject herself to multiple unwanted abortions which can in the long run be even more harmful then multiple unwanted pregnancies.

Myth: Banning sex selective abortions can hamper the family planning programme. Fewer women would mean fewer children.
Reality: Sex-selective abortions have resulted in alarmingly fewer girl children. Any family planning strategy which interferes with the natural sex ratio can have a disastrous effect on society.

Myth: A woman has to pay dowry because she is an economic dependant. A man is the breadwinner. His family pays for his education and upbringing. Therefore, both he and his family have to be adequately compensated for taking on a new economic liability.
Reality: In many cases women are the sole breadwinners. Even when they are highly educated and hold jobs they have to pay dowry. Women doctors, engineers, teachers, nurses and even women agricultural labourers pay dowry. As for full-time homemakers, they are the ones who strategize the proper use of the money, allocate it for food, education, shelter and other important everyday needs. They can in no way be

considered economic liabilities. Families cannot survive without women.

Myth: A high dowry defines a woman's higher status. Women who pay higher dowries are more respected by their in-laws.
Reality: A dowry actually emphasizes the bride's inferior status. 'Inferior' brides pay higher dowries and are more vulnerable to harassment. Dowry 'discounts' are sometimes given to educated or beautiful women. Grooms never pay dowry, however educated or beautiful the bride may be.

Some suggestions:
- Organize a systematic campaign to sensitize doctors and get them to play a proactive role in preventing female foeticide.
- Strictly enforce the PNDT Act and regulate the sale and use of machines and other equipment used for sex-selective abortions.
- Strictly enforce laws pertaining to dowry.
- Attach an economic value to the girl child as well as to the woman. For starters, ensure that social benefits are channelized to a family only through women and girls.
- Have high-powered colourful campaigns to raise the self-esteem of women and to emphasize the fact that they are becoming an endangered species.
- Highlight and publicize the atrocities that are being perpetrated against women in states where there is a shortage.
- Highlight the health backlash on women who have multiple abortions.
- Project the girl child as a social and economic asset.
- Educate young people on the importance of girls and women in society.

- Include topics on basic law pertaining to domestic violence, child abuse, sex-selective abortion and other family related matters in the school curriculum.

Notes

Chapter 1
1. Sen, Amartya, *The New York Review of Books*, 1990.
2. Quoted in *Population and Development Review*,1993.

Chapter 2
1. 'Female Foeticide in Tamil Nadu: Report of the State Level Consultation, Chennai', SIRD, 1998.
2. George, Sabu, 'The Government Response to Female Infanticide in Tamil Nadu: From Recognition Back to Denial.' Paper presented at the 25th Annual MIDS ICSSR Research Methodology Workshop, Kottayam, 1995.

Chapter 3
1. Sen, Amartya, 'More Than a Hundred Million Women Are Missing', *The New York Review of Books*, 1990.
2. ibid.
3. Rummel, R.J., *Death by Government*, Transaction Publishers, 1994.

Chapter 4
1. Quoted by journalist Madhu Gurung in 'The Two-Child Norm Only Leads to Female Foeticide', InfoChange News & Features, November 2004.

2. George, Sabu and Ranbir S. Dahiya , 'Female Foeticide in Rural Haryana', *Economic and Political Weekly*, 1998.
3. Gupte, Manisha, 'Battling Sex Determination', FRCH Newsletter, 1986.

Chapter 8
1. Kaur, Ravinder, 'Mystery of the missing girls', the *Financial Express* (Net edition), August 2005.

Chapter 9
1. Gessell, Arnold, *The Embryology of Behavior: The Beginnings of the Human Mind*, Harper Brothers, 1945.

Chapter 10
1. Sen, Amartya, 'Missing Women Revisited', *British Medical Journal*, 2003.

Bibliography

Census of India 2001

Dagar, Rainuka, *Life Enhancing Mechanisms—Life Depriving Outcomes: A Case of Female Foeticide*, Instititute for Development and Communication, Chandigarh, 2001.

Darnovsky, Marcy, 'Sex Selection Goes Mainstream', *Alter Net,* 2003.

'Diseases by DNA Test', *Indian Journal of Human Genetics,* December 2004.

Dogra, Chander Suta, 'Death Becomes Her', *Outlook,* February 2006.

George, Sabu, 'The Government Response to Female Infanticide in Tamil Nadu: From Recognition Back to Denial', Paper presented at the 25th Annual MIDS ICSSR Research Methodology Workshop, Kottayam, 1995.

Gesell, Arnold, *The Embryology of Behavior: The Beginnings of the Human Mind,* Harper Bros. 1945.

Ginty, Molly, M., 'New Prenatal Tests Raise Hopes and Fears', *WE News,* 2005.

Goldberg, Carey, 'Test Reveals Gender Early in Pregnancy, Ethicists Fear Use in Sex Selection', *Globe Staff,* June 2005.

Gupte, Manisha, 'Battling Sex Determination', *FRCH Newsletter,* 1986.

Gurung, Madhu, 'The Two-Child Norm Only Leads to Female Foeticide', *Infochange India*, 2005.

Hartmann, Betsy, *Sterilization and Abortion, Reproductive Rights and Wrongs: The Global Politics of Population Control*, South End Press, 1995.

Hopson, Janet, L., 'Fetal Psychology', *Psychology Today*, 1998.

Jeeva, M., Gandhimathu and Phavalam, *Female Infanticide: Philisophy,Perspective and Concern of SIRD*, 1998.

Jeeva, M., Phavalam, P., Kanthimathi, A., *Penn Sissu Kolai: Profiles of Victimized Mothers of Female Infanticide* (Tamil), Madurai Society for Integrated Rural Development, 2003.

Klasen, S., Wink, C., 'Missing women: Revisiting the debate', *Feminist Economist,* 2003.

Krishnakumar, Asha., 'Scanning for Death', *Frontline,* 1998.

Kulkarni, Sanjeev, *Radical Journal of Health,* Bombay, 1986.

McDougall, Dan, 'Desperate British Asians Fly to India to Abort Baby Girls', *The Observer,* 2006.

Mehrotra, Ritu, Bhatia, Raminder, 'Sex Prediction Tests and Women's Health', *PUCL Bulletin,* 1982.

Menon, Parvathi and Shobhana Roychoudhary, 'Dubious Choice', *Frontline,* 2001.

Milner, Larry, S., *A Brief History of Infanticide,* Society For the Prevention of Infanticide, 1998.

'Missing': Mapping the Adverse Sex Ratio in India, UNFPA Publication, Delhi, 2003.

Pandey, Chandrakala, 'Son preference in Hindu religious books and traditions', *AIDWA website,* 2002.

Pushkarna, Vijaya, 'Instant Injustice', *The Week,* June 2004.

Rummel, R.J., *Death by Government,* Transaction Publishers, 1994.

Sachs, Susan, 'Clinics' Pitch to Indian Émigrés: It's a Boy',

The New York Times, 2001.

Saha, Biswajit, 'The Diagnostic Potential of Maternal Plasma in Detecting Fetal Diseases by DNA Test', *Saving the Girl Child: A Strategies Manual*, Indian Council for Child Welfare (ICCW), Chennai, 2003.

Sen A.K., 'Many Faces of Gender Inequality', *Frontline*, 2001.

Sen, A.K., 'Missing Women', *British Medical Journal*, 1992.

Sharma, Radha, 'Marriage of Inconvenience', the *Times of India*, 2005.

Singh, Gur Kirpal, 'Punjab Docs Abort Male Foetuses For A Quick Buck', the *Times of India*, May 2005.

Sudha, S., S. Khanna, Rajan S. Irudaya and Roma Srivastava, 'Traditions in Transformation: Gender Bias among the Nairs of Kerala', *Seminar on Female Deficit in Asia: Trends and Perspectives*, Singapore, 2005.

Tendulkar, Vijay, Teesta Setalvad and Ammu Abraham, 'Where Are Our Girls?', Press Note Issued by Centre For Justice and Peace and Women's Centre, June 2005.

'The Laws of Manu, c.1500 BCE' (translated by G. Buhler), *Indian History Sourcebook*.

Varghese, Joe, Vijay Aruldas and Jeemon Panniyammakal, 'Analysis of Trends in Sex Ratio at Birth of Hospitalized Deliveries in the State of Delhi', *Christian Medical Association of India*, 2005.

Visaria, Leela, 'Female Deficit in India: Role of Prevention of Sex Selective Abortion Act', *Seminar on Female Deficit in Asia: Trends and Perspectives*, Singapore, 2005.

Index

sterilization, monetary incentives
for, 36
stree dhanam, 163
Suction Curettage (or Vacuum
Aspiration), 150
Sweden, 154; women, 156, 157

Tamil Nadu
female infanticide and foeticide,
96, 99
sex ratios, 164
State Women's Commission
(SWC), 35
women deficit, 162
technological advancements,
see medical technology
tharavadu, 155–59, 161
Thevars, 24
trans-vaginal scans, 66
trauma of multiple illegal
abortions, 87–88

ultrasonography/ultrasound, 68,
76, 94–95, 97
centers and decline in child sex
ratio, co-relation, 68–69
as a diagnostic and therapeutic
tool, 65, 69
for sex selection, 68–69
UNICEF, 3
United Kingdom National Health
Scheme (NHS), 76–77
United Nations Population Fund
(UNFPA), 39, 147
United States: missing women, 42
Uttar Pradesh: women deficit, 49
urban Child Sex Ratio (CSR), 45–
46

Usilampatti, Madurai, Tamil
Nadu, 1, 8, 73, 111, 167
Cradle Babies' scheme, 4
female infanticide, 2–7, 20, 21,
25, 26, 29, 38, 40 sex selective
scanning, 66
women' self-reliance, 29

Vaigai irrigation project, 15–16
Vakria, Ila, 135
Vannars, 24
varadatchinai, *see* dowry
Vimochana, 71–72
violence, 118–20
against women, 35, 46
Visaria, Dr Leela, 66, 98–100
visiting husband, 154–56
see also Nairs
Voluntary Health Association of
India (VHAI), 100

women, women's, 9
anatomy, 144
atrocities on, 65
bias against, *see* gender bias
commoditization, 16
deficit, 48–49, 162
democratic right of freedom of
choice, 82
dependent, 50–51
devaluation, 17
disempowerment, 7, 8, 10, 12,
18, 25, 27, 34–35, 88, 90,
116, 124–25, 173
inheritance rights, 156–59,
161
marginalization, 15
participation in economic